Second International Workshop on Automatic Translation for Signed and Spoken Languages (AT4SSL 2023)

Sign Language Parallel Data - Challenges, Solutions and Resolutions

Tampere, Finland
15 June 2023

Editors:

Dimitar Shterionov
Mirella De Sisto
Mathias Muller
Davy Van Landuyt
Rehana Omardeen
Shaun Oboyle
Annelies Braffort
Floris Roelofsen
Frederic Blain
Bram Vanroy
Eleftherios Avramidis

ISBN: 978-1-7138-8994-6

Printed from e-media with permission by:

Curran Associates, Inc.
57 Morehouse Lane
Red Hook, NY 12571

CURRAN ASSOCIATES INC.
proceedings.com

Some format issues inherent in the e-media version may also appear in this print version.

Association for Computational Linguistics
209 N. Eighth Street
Stroudsburg, Pennsylvania 18360

Phone: 1-570-476-8006
Fax: 1-570-476-0860

acl@aclweb.org

Additional copies of this publication are available from:

Curran Associates, Inc.
57 Morehouse Lane
Red Hook, NY 12571 USA
Phone: 845-758-0400
Fax: 845-758-2633
Email: curran@proceedings.com
Web: www.proceedings.com

AT4SSL

Proceedings of the

Second International Workshop on Automatic Translation for Signed and Spoken Languages

15 June 2023

Edited by

Dimitar Shterionov, Mirella De Sisto, Mathias Müller, Davy Van Landuyt, Rehana Omardeen, Shaun Oboyle, Annelies Braffort, Floris Roelofsen, Frédéric Blain, Bram Vanroy and Eleftherios Avramidis

DOI: 10.26116/t9eb-fr769789464857184

Published by Open Press Tilburg University
Tilburg, the Netherlands
https://www.openpresstiu.org

OPEN PRESS TiU

Contents

Preface by the Workshop Organizers

This volume contains the proceedings of the Second International Workshop on Automatic Translation for Sign and Spoken Languages (AT4SSL 2023)[1], hosted by the 24th Annual Conference of The European Association for Machine Translation (EAMT 2023)[2]. This workshop is a venue for presenting and discussing (complete, ongoing or future) research on automatic translation between sign and spoken languages.

AT4SSL 2021 The first edition of the AT4SSL workshop[3] was co-located with the AMTA conference in 2021. The workshop was conducted online, featured eight long papers, presenting completed work, and three short papers, presenting ongoing work were accepted for presentation, and was attended by approximately 35 participants.

AT4SSL 2023 scope and theme The main theme of the 2023 edition of the AT4SSL workshop is *Sign language parallel data – challenges, solutions and resolutions*: Data is one of the key factors for the success of today's AI, including language and translation models for sign and spoken languages. However, when it comes to processing sign language and training machine-learning systems we face the problems of small volumes of (parallel) data, large veracity in terms of origin of annotations (deaf or hearing interpreters), non-standardized annotations (e.g. glosses differ across corpora), video quality or recording setting, and others. In this edition of the workshop we focus on the discussion of data quantity, data quality, (re)sources, ethical and ownership concerns.

Submissions and programme The workshop welcomed two types of contributions: long and short research papers. AT4SSL 2023 received a total of 9 new submissions (4 long and 5 short papers). Following the peer-review process, 6 submissions were accepted (3 long and 3 short papers), resulting in an acceptance rate of 67% that highlights the quality of the submissions received.

The accepted papers cover a diverse range of topics related to automatic translation between signed and spoken languages, and focus on data resources, linguistics and machine translation

[1] `https://sites.google.com/tilburguniversity.edu/at4ssl2023/home`

[2] `https://events.tuni.fi/eamt23/`

[3] Dimitar Shterionov, ed. *Proceedings of the 1st International Workshop on Automatic Translation for Signed and Spoken Languages (AT4SSL)*. Virtual: Association for Machine Translation in the Americas, Aug. 2021. URL: `https://aclanthology.org/2021.mtsummit-at4ssl.0`.

(MT) systems. The papers by McGill, E. and Saggion, H., and by De Sisto, M. et al. present new sign language corpora for BSL, VGT and NGT; the paper by Declerck, T. et al. present a unified RDF-based representation for various type of data aiming to facilitate a common signed and spoken language repository; Moryoseff, A. et al. present in their paper a new baseline MT based on a transformation from text to glosses to poses and to video in the context of translation into SL for DGS. The work presented by the paper of Hollain, N. et al. investigates the use of approximative linguistic features for sign language processing, seeking improvements over landmark-based features; the paper by Mohammed, Z. and Murtagh, I. presents their work on integrating gerunds of Irish SL in a computational lexicon framework.

In this works we feature two keynote speakers: Vincent Vandeghinste (INT, The Netherlands) and Mathias Müller (UZH, Switzerland) who will talk about general challenges related to sign language data and its use within current NLP tools, and the processing of the JWSigning corpus, respectively. In addition, a round table discussion will facilitate an open discussion between the attendees of the workshop centred around the topic: *The gap between MT for spoken and MT for signed languages: data and technology challenges.*

SignON and EASIER This workshop is organised jointly by members of the SignON (`www.signon-project.eu`) and EASIER (`www.project-easier.eu`) projects. Both SignON and EASIER are Horizon 2020 projects, funded under the Horizon 2020 program ICT-57-2020 - "An empowering, inclusive, Next Generation Internet" with Grant Agreement number 101017255 and 101016982 respectively.

We sincerely thank everyone that contributed to this edition of the AT4SSL workshop: the authors of the submitted papers for their interest in the topic; the Programme Committee members for their valuable feedback and insightful comments; the EAMT organizers for their support.

We hope you enjoy reading the papers and we are looking forward to a fruitful and enriching workshop!

June 2023,
D. Shterionov, M. De Sisto, M. Müller, D. Van Landuyt, R. Omardeen, S. Oboyle, A. Braffort, F. Roelofsen, F. Blain, B. Vanroy, E. Avramidis

AT4SSL 2023 Committees

Organising Committee & Workshop Chairs

Dimitar Shterionov, Department Cognitive Science and Artificial Intelligence, School of Humanities and Digital Sciences, Tilburg University, The Netherlands
Mirella De Sisto, Department Cognitive Science and Artificial Intelligence, School of Humanities and Digital Sciences, Tilburg University, The Netherlands
Mathias Müller, Department of Computational Linguistics, University of Zurich, Switzerland
Davy Van Landuyt, European Union of the Deaf, Belgium
Rehana Omardeen, European Union of the Deaf, Belgium
Shaun O'Boyle, Dublin City University, Ireland
Annelies Braffort, LISN, CNRS, Université Paris-Saclay, France
Floris Roelofsen, Institute for Logic, Language, and Computation, University of Amsterdam, The Netherlands
Frédéric Blain, Department Cognitive Science and Artificial Intelligence, School of Humanities and Digital Sciences, Tilburg University, The Netherlands
Bram Vanroy, Faculty of Arts and Philosophy, Ghent University, Faculty of Arts, KU Leuven, Belgium
Eleftherios Avramidis, German Research Center for Artificial Intelligence (DFKI), Germany

Programme Committee

Ioannis Tsochantaridis, Google Research, Switzerland
Amit Moryossef, Department of Computer ScienceBar-Ilan University, Israel
Lyke Esselink, Faculty of ScienceUniversity of Amsterdam, The Netherlands
Jampierre Rocha, Lenovo, Brazil
Mathieu De Coster, IDLab-AIROGhent University, Belgium
Myriam Vermeerbergen, Faculty of Arts, Katholieke Universiteit Leuven, Belgium
Amanda Duarte, Image Processing Group, Signal Theory and Communications DepartmentUniversitat Politècnica de Catalunya, Spain
Silvia Rodríguez Vázquez, Department of Translation Technology, Faculty of Translation and InterpretingUniversity of Geneva, Switzerland
Giacomo Inches, Martel Innovate, Switzerland
Cristina España-Bonet, Universität de Saarlandes, German Research Center for Artificial Intelligence (DFKI), Germany
Ahmet Alp Kindiroglu, Perceptual Intelligence Laboratory (PILAB), Department of Computer Engineering, Bogazici Universitesi, Turkey
Sarah Ebling, Department of Computational Linguistics, University of Zurich, Switzerland

Workshop Program

Time	Activity
09:00	**Start of the workshop**
09:00 – 09:15	**Opening notes**
09:15 – 10:30	**Keynote 1:** *Challenges with Sign Language Datasets* Vincent Vandeghinste (INT) **Keynote 2:** *JWSign: A Highly Multilingual Corpus of Bible Translations for Sign Language Processing* Mathias Müller (UZH)
10:30 – 11:00	Coffee break
11:00 – 12:30	**Presentation Session 1**
	Analyzing the Potential of Linguistic Features for Sign Spotting: A Look at Approximative Features Natalie Hollain, Martha Larson and Floris Roelofsen
	A Linked Data Approach for linking and aligning Sign Language and Spoken Language Data Thierry Declerck, Sam Bigeard, Fahad Khan, Irene Murtagh, Sussi Olsen, Mike Rosner, Ineke Schuurman, Andon Tchechmedjiev and Andy Way
	An Open-Source Gloss-Based Baseline for Spoken to Signed Language Translation Amit Moryossef, Mathias Müller, Anne Göhring, Zifan Jiang, Yoav Goldberg and Sarah Ebling
12:30 – 13:30	Lunch break
13:30 – 15:00	**Round table** *The gap between MT for spoken and MT for signed languages: data and technology challenges* Moderator: Mathias Müller (UZH)
15:00 – 15:30	Coffee break
15:30 – 17:00	**Presentation Session 2**
	A New English-Dutch-NGT Corpus for the Hospitality Domain Mirella De Sisto, Vincent Vandeghinste and Dimitar Shterionov
	BSL-Hansard: A parallel, multimodal corpus of English and interpreted British Sign Language data from parliamentary proceedings Euan McGill and Horacio Saggion
	Towards Accommodating Gerunds within the Sign Language Lexicon Zaid Mohammed and Irene Murtagh
17:00 – 17:15	**Closing remarks**
17:15	**End of the workshop**

Long Papers

Analyzing the Potential of Linguistic Features for Sign Spotting: A Look at Approximative Features

Natalie Hollain
Institute for Computing
and Information Sciences
Radboud University
natalie.hollain@ru.nl

Martha Larson
Center for Language Studies
and Institute for Computing
and Information Sciences
Radboud University
martha.larson@ru.nl

Floris Roelofsen
Institute for Logic,
Language and Computation
University of Amsterdam
f.roelofsen@uva.nl

Abstract

Sign language processing is the field of research that aims to recognize, retrieve, and spot signs in videos. Various approaches have been developed, varying in whether they use linguistic features and whether they use landmark detection tools or not. Incorporating linguistics holds promise for improving sign language processing in terms of performance, generalizability, and explainability. This paper focuses on the task of sign spotting and aims to expand on the approximative linguistic features that have been used in previous work, and to understand when linguistic features deliver an improvement over landmark features. We detect landmarks with Mediapipe and extract linguistically relevant features from them, including handshape, orientation, location, and movement. We compare a sign spotting model using linguistic features with a model operating on landmarks directly, finding that the approximate linguistic features tested in this paper capture some aspects of signs better than the landmark features, while they are worse for others.

1 Introduction

Sign Language Processing (SLP) (Bragg et al., 2019; Moryossef and Goldberg, 2021) is the field of research that studies how signs and signed phrases can be recognized, retrieved and spotted in videos. Key approaches differ with respect to whether they attempt to leverage linguistics/phonology, and the way in which they do it, as shown in Figure 1. Some recent work used pixel information as input (Approach **A**) without explicitly considering linguistic features that are relevant for sign language (e.g. handshape and orientation of the hand) (Momeni et al., 2020; Jiang et al., 2021). On the other hand, earlier work in sign language recognition proposed methods to extract phonological properties of signs from pixel information (Bowden et al., 2004; Von Agris et al., 2008; Han et al., 2009; Zaki and Shaheen, 2011) (Approach **B**). Other approaches have applied a landmark detection tool, such as OpenPose, to obtain the location of landmarks in the body from the pixel input and used them to train a model (Ko et al., 2018; Ko et al., 2019) (Approach **C**). Angle and distance features which approximate the phonological properties of a sign have also been extracted from these landmarks (Shin et al., 2021; Hussain et al., 2022; Farhan and Madi, 2022) (Approach **D**). SLP research seeks to use approximative features where possible to avoid the computational overhead of calculating features that reflect linguistic properties exactly. An approximation is considered sufficiently good if it contributes to the performance of an SLP system.

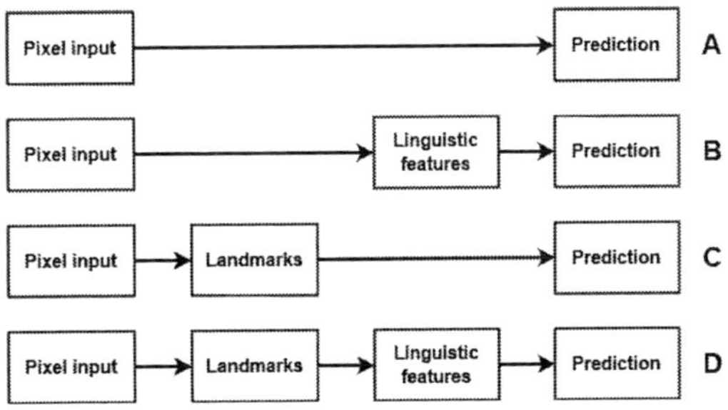

Figure 1: Four methods for sign language processing

Incorporating linguistic features holds great promise for improving SLP in terms of generalizability and explainability. The drawback of incorporating linguistic features based on pixel information, as in Approach B, is that this method is sensitive to particular properties of the training data, such as the lighting conditions, the skin colour of the signer, the color and shape of the signer's clothes, and the recording background. Approach D, which we pursue here, improves on this by implementing a modular approach which is potentially more robust because linguistic features are extracted from landmarks rather than pixel input.

The purpose of this paper is to move research adopting Approach D beyond the current state of the art. We make two contributions. First, we expand the inventory of approximative linguistic features that are used for SLP. Second, we seek to understand when linguistic features deliver an improvement over the landmark features from which they are produced. In contrast, previous work solely focused on the ability of linguistic features to improve performance of SLP systems and did not examine what makes these features important.

The reason why linguistic features extracted from landmarks can be anticipated to be more robust is that the modularity of this approach makes it possible to use existing tools for landmark detection, such as Mediapipe (Zhang et al., 2020), OpenPose (Cao et al., 2017), or MMPose (Sengupta et al., 2020). Mediapipe, for instance, has been trained on a large-scale, in-the-wild dataset (as well as curated and synthetic data) with high variability in background, lighting conditions, the skin colour of subjects, and other visual artifacts. In addition, the modular nature of the approach makes it straightforward to incorporate future improvements of landmark detection technologies as they become available.

This paper focuses on the task of sign *spotting*, which has as its goal to determine when a given target sign occurs in a video of continuous signing. Sign spotting is distinct from sign recognition, because we need to establish *when* a sign occurs in a given video. Recognition only uses video segments in which one isolated sign is performed.

Building on the aforementioned work in sign language recognition (SLR) (Shin et al., 2021; Hussain et al., 2022; Farhan and Madi, 2022), we first detect landmarks with Mediapipe and then extract linguistically relevant features from these landmarks. In the extraction phase, we expand on previous work in that we do not only extract features that serve as an approximate representation of the handshape of the signer, but also features that correspond to other relevant properties, such as the orientation of the hand, its location relative to the body, and its movement through space.

We compare a sign spotting model which makes use of these approximative linguistic features with one that operates on landmarks directly (approach **D** and **C**, respectively). We find that the approximate linguistic features tested in this paper capture some aspects of signs better than the landmark features, while they are worse for others. Our code is made available on Github[1].

2 Background

2.1 Sign language phonology and phonetics

Sign language phonology studies the articulation of signs within and across different sign languages. Typically, the phonological properties of a sign are split up into manual and non-manual properties. Non-manual properties pertain to the face, in particular the mouth, and the signer's body posture (Pendzich, 2020). Manual phonological properties pertain to the shape, orientation, location and movement of the signer's hands (Stokoe, 1960; Battison, 1978; Van der Kooij, 2002; Sandler, 2012; Brentari et al., 2018; Brentari, 2019). We focus here on manual phonological properties.

The phonology of a sign is not the only factor that influences how the sign is articulated in reality. The specific characteristics of the signer, such as their emotional state, language background, age and gender, can change how signs are performed in practice. Moreover, the linguistic context in which the sign is uttered, in particular the previous and subsequent sign, is an important factor in a sign's articulation. The concrete realisation of signs, as influenced by these factors and more, is studied in the field of sign language phonetics (Crasborn, 2012; Tyrone, 2020). In this work, we focus on the basic phonological parameters that we introduced above, leaving the study of phonetics to future work.

2.2 Sign spotting

We give a brief overview of notable work on sign spotting before describing what distinguishes our

[1] https://github.com/nataliehh/Linguistic-Features-for-Sign-Spotting

work from what has already been done. A variety of methods have been applied in previous work, including dynamic time warping (Viitaniemi et al., 2014), conditional random fields (Cho et al., 2009; Yang and Lee, 2010), hierarchical sequential patterns (Ong et al., 2014) and hidden Markov models (Elmezain et al., 2008). Typically, these approaches were applied to datasets that only contained a small set of signs and signers. More recently, the focus has been on the application of deep learning methods, such as 3D convolution (Jiang et al., 2021; Wong et al., 2023; Enriquez et al., 2022).

We highlight in particular the work of Momeni et al. (2020), which proposed a framework for continuous sign spotting called 'watch, read and lookup'. A model was trained to create sign spotting embeddings using sparsely annotated videos and examples from a video dictionary of signs. The authors use BSL-1k, a dataset that contains videos of BBC broadcasts that have been interpreted in sign language. Interpreted signing is distinct from 'natural signing', the latter being faster and less distinctly signed (Bragg et al., 2019).

Our work contrasts with current approaches to sign spotting, which either used ad-hoc datasets or operated directly on pixel input. We use a dataset which matches most of the criteria described by Bragg et al. (2019). Furthermore, although linguistic features have been used for other SLP tasks, we are the first to our knowledge to investigate their potential for sign spotting.

3 Method

3.1 Data

We use the Corpus Nederlandse Gebarentaal (CNGT) (Crasborn and Zwitserlood, 2008; Crasborn et al., 2008) to train our sign spotting model. It contains 72 hours of video footage of 104 signers conversing in Dutch Sign Language (NGT), recorded at 25 fps. Circa 15% of the corpus is annotated, which is equivalent to 162k annotations of 3.2k unique signs. CNGT is annotated using NGT Signbank (Crasborn et al., 2014), which contains information about the phonological properties of signs discussed in Section 2.1.

The corpus consists of videos of 'natural' signing, where signers are in conversation and are not signing in a more proper manner than usual (Crasborn and Zwitserlood, 2008). The dataset contains footage that is compatible with real-world applications (Bragg et al., 2019), and contains a large amount of different signs and signers. Thus, CNGT forms a good basis for SLP applications.

We prepare the data of CNGT for our model as follows. First, we split the annotations into a train, validation and test set. We ensure that the training set does not contain the same signers as the validation or test set to make our system signer-independent. We filter out signs which are not seen during training, as well as signs for which no linguistic information is available in the NGT Lexicon in Signbank, since we require such information for our performance analysis. After this preprocessing step, 118k annotations of 2.7k unique signs remain. We use a data split of approximately 80/10/10, with 90k train, 10.5k validation and 9.5k test annotations.

To create more variety in the training set, we augment it by mirroring the footage. This is done to ensure that one-handed signs occur signed with both the right and the left hand. Similarly, two-handed signs where one hand is dominant now also occur with each hand being dominant. After the augmentation, we have 180k train instances. We found that our model converges more consistently with this augmentation than without it.

Due to the fact that signs have variability in how long they are signed, the annotations in our dataset are of variable length. Thus, to make the input compatible with a neural network architecture, we ensure that our inputs are transformed to a fixed length. We select a target length of 10 frames, which is equal to the mean duration of the annotations in the corpus. Annotations that are shorter than 10 frames are simply padded with zeros to the target length. For annotations that are too long, we undersample to 10 frames.

3.2 Landmark detection

For each frame of our dataset, we detect landmarks on the hands and body using Mediapipe. Each hand has 21 landmarks, as shown in Figure 2. While Mediapipe is capable of estimating the x, y, z coordinates of each landmark, the z coordinate is less reliable. As such, we only make use of the 2D coordinates, x and y.

Mediapipe normalises landmarks using the video dimensions (width and height), which means that landmark coordinates are not comparable across videos with different dimensions. Therefore, we reverse the dimension-wise normalisation

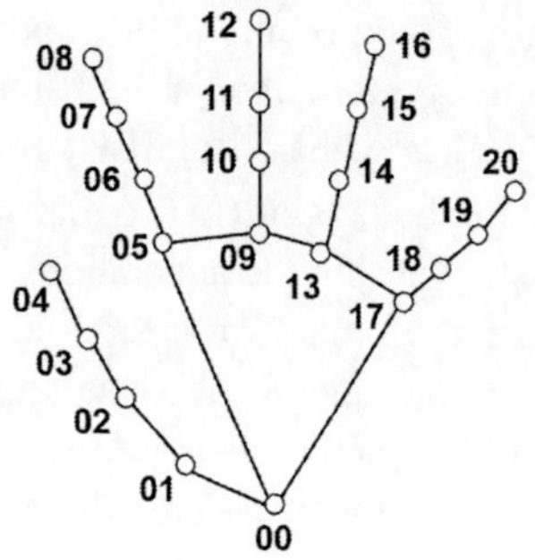

Figure 2: The 21 Mediapipe landmarks for one hand

to convert them back to pixel coordinates. In other words, given a landmark with normalised coordinates $[x, y]$ in a video with dimensions w, h, we perform the operation $[x \cdot w, y \cdot h]$.

After reversing the normalisation, we apply the normalisation described by Celebi et al. (2013). For each frame, we obtain the landmarks of the left and right shoulder, sh_L and sh_R. Every landmark ℓ at a given frame is then normalised as follows:

- We scale ℓ using the absolute distance between the shoulders: $\dfrac{\ell}{\text{abs}(\text{sh}_L - \text{sh}_R)}$
- We center ℓ by subtracting the midpoint of the shoulders: $\ell - \dfrac{\text{abs}(\text{sh}_L + \text{sh}_R)}{2}$.

For our model that uses landmark features, we simply use the normalised landmarks of both hands as our input, or $21 \cdot 2 = 42$ landmarks. Each landmark consists of an x and y coordinate, such that we use $42 \cdot 2 = 84$ features for each frame by using all of the coordinates as features. Thus, each annotation results in a data input of shape $(10, 84)$.

3.3 Linguistic features

To represent the basic phonological parameters, we extracted the following types of features from the normalised landmarks:

- Handshape: the distances and angles between the fingertips, handpalm and wrist.
- Orientation: the angle of the handpalm relative to the torso and the shoulders.
- Location: the x, y coordinates of the wrist(s) and fingertips.
- Movement: the velocity of the wrist.

The handshape angle features are computed using a start, middle and end point triple, (ℓ_s, ℓ_m, ℓ_e), and the arctangent measure:

$$\text{angle}(\ell_s, \ell_m, \ell_e) = \text{atan2}(\ell_{e,y} - \ell_{m,y}, \ell_{e,x} - \ell_{m,x}) - \text{atan2}(\ell_{s,y} - \ell_{m,y}, \ell_{s,x} - \ell_{m,x})$$

where we indicate with the subscript whether the x, y coordinate of the element is used, e.g. $\ell_{1,x}$ indicates the x coordinate of landmark ℓ_1.

For each finger, we compute the angle with the wrist as well as its internal angle. For instance, we get the angle within the thumb using landmarks $[01, 02, 04]$ and get the thumb's angle with the wrist using $[00, 01, 04]$.

For the handshape distance features, we calculate the Euclidean distance between pairs of landmarks ℓ_1, ℓ_2:

$$\text{dist}(\ell_1, \ell_2) = \sqrt{(\ell_{1,x} - \ell_{2,x})^2 + (\ell_{1,y} - \ell_{2,y})^2}$$

To compute the hand orientation, we use Mediapipe's Pose model, which captures the position of landmarks of the entire body. In particular, we use the landmarks of the left shoulder sh_L (pose index 11), right shoulder sh_R (index 12), left hip hip_L (index 23) and right hip hip_R (index 24). We draw two lines using these landmarks: the horizontal line between the shoulders, $(\text{sh}_L, \text{sh}_R)$, and the vertical line in the middle of the torso, $(\dfrac{\text{sh}_L + \text{sh}_R}{2}, \dfrac{\text{hip}_L + \text{hip}_R}{2})$. For the landmarks within the hand, we draw two axes within the hand: one between index 00 and 09, the y-axis, and one between 05 and 17, the x-axis.

Based on the lines that have been drawn for the shoulders, torso and hands, we now compute the slope of each line. For a given line ℓ that consists of a start and end point (ℓ_s, ℓ_e), we compute the slope s_ℓ of the line as:

$$s_\ell = \frac{\ell_{e,y} - \ell_{s,y}}{\ell_{e,x} - \ell_{s,x}}$$

Finally, we can compute the angle between two lines for which we computed the slopes, s_1, s_2:

$$\text{angle}(s_1, s_2) = \arctan(\frac{s_2 - s_1}{1 + (s_2 \cdot s_1)})$$

The hand orientation is then represented by the angles between the x-axis and y-axis of the hand with the shoulders and with the torso. We do not compare the angle of the torso and shoulders, nor the x-axis and y-axis of the hand because these are not relevant for the orientation of the hand relative to the body. As such, we end up with four distinct orientation angles.

Feature Ind.	Type	Ind. Mediapipe Landmarks
0 – 24	Handshape (Angles)	[01,02,04], [00,01,04], [05,06,08], [00,05,08], [09,10,12], [00,09,12], [13,14,16], [00,13,16], [17,18,20], [00,17,20], **[02,03,04]**, **[05,06,07]**, **[06,07,08]**, **[09,10,11]**, **[10,11,12]**, **[13,14,15]**, **[14,15,16]**, **[17,18,19]**, **[18,19,20]**, **[04,00,08]**, **[08,00,20]**, **[16,17,20]**, **[08,05,12]**, **[04,05,20]**, **[08,13,20]**
25 – 39	Handshape (Distances)	[00,04], [00,08], [00,12], [00,16], [00,20], [04,08], [04,12], [04,16], [04,20], [08,12], [08,16], [08,20], [12,16], [12,20], [16,20]
40 – 43	Hand orientation	[00,09], [05,17] + Pose: [11, 12, 23, 24]
44 – 55	Wrist, fingertip locations	00, 04, 08, 12, 16, 20
56 – 58	Wrist velocity	00
59 – 117	Features other hand	*See features 0 – 58*
118 – 119	Distance between wrists	00

Table 1: Feature indices

The location of the hand is simply represented using the x, y coordinates of the wrist and the fingertips. To capture the movement of the hand, we compute the velocity of the wrist. We do this in three different ways: first, we compute the Euclidean distance between the location of the wrist at the current frame and the last frame. This is done in the same manner as for the handshape distance features. Second, we separately store the difference between the x coordinate of the wrist between these two frames. We do the same for the y coordinate to obtain the third feature. This way, we capture both an average velocity that combines the x, y coordinates, as well as the horizontal and vertical velocity.

Finally, we capture the horizontal and vertical distance between the wrists of the hands. These features are chosen because the location of a sign is partially characterised by the interaction between the hands. We compute the difference between the x and y coordinates, resulting in two features.

In Table 1, the extracted features are displayed. The *Ind. Mediapipe Landmarks* column shows which indices from the Mediapipe hand model are used, while the *Feature Ind.* column indicates the indices of our created features. Note that the shown indices are only for the left hand. The right hand's indices are equivalent modulo 59, e.g. the first feature of the right hand that computes the angle for landmark indices $[01, 02, 04]$, is at index 59. In total, we use 120 features to represent the phonological properties of both hands.

Some of the extracted features are adapted from previous work. **Bold** values indicate features taken from Farhan et al. (2022). All distance features are adopted from Shin et al. (2021). The remaining features are novel.

3.4 Model architecture

Based on Momeni et al. (2020), we develop a model which learns to create embeddings from our input features, such that inputs of the same sign result in similar embeddings while inputs of different signs result in dissimilar embeddings. The model that we chose for our experiments is a LSTM network. LSTMs can extract temporal information from data sequences and have been a popular tool for natural language processing (Chai and Li, 2019). While more sophisticated architectures are available these days, our goal is not to select the best model but rather to engineer meaningful features. We tested multiple configurations of our network and selected one which performs well for both the landmark and linguistic features. Our chosen configuration is shown in Figure 3.

We start with a masking layer to deal with our zero padding, followed by a Gaussian noise layer which creates variability in our data to make the model generalize better. We empirically found that a standard deviation of $\sigma = 0.001$ for the noise is suitable. It is followed by a biLSTM layer with $2 \cdot 128 = 256$ nodes, and two dense layers of size 256. We use batch normalization between the dense layers for training stability. A batch size of

```
Layer (type)                 Output Shape              Param #
=================================================================
masking (Masking)            (None, 10, 84)            0

gaussian_noise (GaussianNoi  (None, 10, 84)            0
se)

bidirectional (Bidirectiona  (None, 256)               218112
l)

dense (Dense)                (None, 256)               65792

batch_normalization (BatchN  (None, 256)               1024
ormalization)

dense_1 (Dense)              (None, 256)               65792

=================================================================
Total params: 350,720
Trainable params: 350,208
Non-trainable params: 512
```

Figure 3: Model architecture

128 and learning rate of 0.001 are used, inspired by Momeni et al. (2020). We train the model using the Adam optimizer for 10 epochs, which is when it typically starts to converge on the validation set. Due to the strength of contrastive loss reported in the literature (e.g. (Momeni et al., 2020)), we apply supervised contrastive loss to train our model (Khosla et al., 2020).

3.5 Experimental setup

Our experiments compare our expanded inventory of approximative linguistic features against a pipeline using only Mediapipe landmarks. Our main goal is to investigate when linguistic features contribute to sign spotting performance. We train two sign spotting models, one using the linguistic features extracted from the landmarks and the other using the landmark features directly. In order to test our models, we move a sliding window with the same size as our train inputs, 10 frames, over our test set videos. For each window and for each target sign, we compute their cosine distance d. The inventory of target signs consists of all 1038 signs present in the test set. If d is lower or equal to our spotting threshold τ, i.e. $d \leq \tau$, we say the target sign has been spotted. We report our results at $\tau = 0.2$ for both models, which we empirically found to be a good spotting threshold on the validation set.

Each target sign has been seen multiple times during training. As such, using each train embedding individually to find the spottings in a test video requires many comparisons. To reduce the number of comparisons, we create *reference embeddings* for each sign. For a sign S, we first compute embeddings of its training set occurrences. These embeddings are then compared to each other in terms of their cosine distance to each other. We investigate which the embeddings are, on average, closest to all other embeddings of S, and define them to be most representative of S. The top 10% most representative embeddings are averaged to make one reference embedding for S. The predicted spottings of a sign S can then be found using the reference embeddings.

3.6 Evaluation

In this section, we describe how we evaluate the two models. Recall that we aim to achieve insight into when linguistic features are contributing to sign spotting. To this end, our evaluation approach makes use of *confusable signs*: signs which only differ from a given target by a single phonological property. For instance, a pair of signs may only differ in where they are signed, in which case they form confusable signs for each other based on location. We call the single property that differs between the confusable signs the *Δ property*. By investigating which confusable signs are actually mistaken for a given target sign, we are able to discover which phonological properties are difficult to distinguish using each set of features.

We evaluate our sign spotting models by computing the true positive (TP), false negative (FN), true negative (TN) and false positive (FP) evaluations for each model. The FP and TN evaluations are computed by obtaining the confusable signs for each target sign that are present in our test set videos. The confusable signs are selected based on the linguistic properties provided by NGT Signbank (Crasborn et al., 2020).

We begin by analyzing the confusable signs for each target sign and determining their Δ properties. In Table 2, the frequency of the Δ properties in our test set is shown. Notably, a few Δ properties are much more common than others. This may be related to how many confusable signs exist with a particular Δ property. For example, there may be few signs for which only the handshape of the weak hand differs from another sign. Additionally, if confusable signs with a given Δ property are not common signs in our corpus, the Δ property will also not occur frequently.

The TP, FN, TN and FP instances are calculated using *tolerance to irrelevance* (TTI) (De Vries et al., 2004). This metric is based on the assumption that users, when given an entry point in an audio or video stream, keep listening or watching until their tolerance to irrelevant content has been

Δ property	Test set frequency
Alternating Movement	182
Contact Type	231
Handedness	4263
Handshape Change	299
Location	18078
Movement Direction	16566
Movement Shape	749
Orientation Change	568
Relation between Articulators	42
Relative Orientation: Location	1711
Relative Orientation: Movement	2839
Repeated Movement	1047
Strong Hand	35043
Weak Hand	85

Table 2: Frequency of Δ properties in our test set

reached. TTI is thus relevant to our evaluation, as sign spotting systems should reflect real-life applications (Bragg et al., 2019).

To capture a user's tolerance, TTI makes use of a *tolerance window* which allows for entry points to be located a bit before or at the start of the relevant content, but not after it has begun. The reasoning behind this decision is that it has been found to be annoying to users when entry points are given after the start of the relevant section (He et al., 1999).

We formalize TTI for our analysis as follows. For a given ground truth annotation s_j, a TP occurs when a prediction p_i, with onset time t_{p_i}, falls into its tolerance window:

$$t_{pi} \in [t_{s_j} - tol, t_{s_j}]$$

where t_{s_j} is the onset time of s_j. In contrast, a FN occurs when no prediction falls into this tolerance window. The tolerance tol can be chosen depending on the exact context in which TTI is used. There are currently no established tolerance levels for SLP, thus, we consult the related field of audio segmentation for our tolerance. We found $tol = 0.5$ seconds to be a frequently used tolerance for audio (Aljanaki et al., 2015; Smith and Chew, 2013; Smith et al., 2011).

To compute the FP and TN instances, we obtain the confusable signs, $C(S)$, for each target sign S:

$$C(S) = \{A, B, ..., Z\}$$

We then determine when the confusable signs are annotated in CNGT:

$$ANN_{C(S)} = \{A_1, ..., A_m, ..., Z_1, ..., Z_n\}$$

Next, we select the onset time of each confusable sign annotation:

$$T_{ANN_{C(S)}} = \{t_{A_1}, ..., t_{A_m}, ..., t_{Z_1}, ..., t_{Z_n}\}$$

Based on the notation above, we can then define FP and TN evaluations. Given the onset time of an annotation for a confusable sign, $t_{c_j} \in T_{ANN_{C(S)}}$, and a set of predictions $P(S)$ with onset times $T_{P(S)}$, we define the FP and TN evaluations as:

$$FP(t_{c_j}) \text{ iff } \exists t_{p_i} \in T_{P(S)} : t_{pi} \in [t_{c_j} - tol, t_{c_j}]$$
$$TN(t_{c_j}) \text{ iff } \forall t_{pi} \in T_{P(S)} : t_{pi} \notin [t_{c_j} - tol, t_{c_j}]$$

In other words, a predicted spotting of a given target is a FP if it falls within the tolerance window of an annotated occurrence of another sign that is a confusable sign for the target. On the other hand, a TN occurs if we do *not* predict a spotting within the tolerance window of this annotated occurrence of the confusable sign.

Finally, we can analyze the FP and TN instances in terms of their Δ properties to determine which phonological properties are difficult to distinguish for our model. Our general approach to evaluating sign spotting models is further elaborated elsewhere (Hollain et al., 2023).

4 Results

The results of our evaluation are shown in Table 3. The model that was trained with the linguistic features produces more TP spottings than the model trained using landmarks, as well as fewer FP instances for the confusable signs.

Model	TP	FN	FP	TN
Linguistic	5442	4274	11395	68263
Landmarks	5380	4336	12292	67366

Table 3: Performance using linguistic and landmark features

We now investigate the capabilities of our linguistic features to capture the linguistic properties of signs, compared to the landmark features. In Figure 4, we display the percentage of FPs per Δ property. The percentage is computed by counting how often the confusable signs with each Δ property, as shown in Table 2, are falsely spotted. For instance, a value of 50% in the Alternating Movement column would indicate that $182 \cdot 0.5 = 91$ of the confusable signs that differ only in this Δ

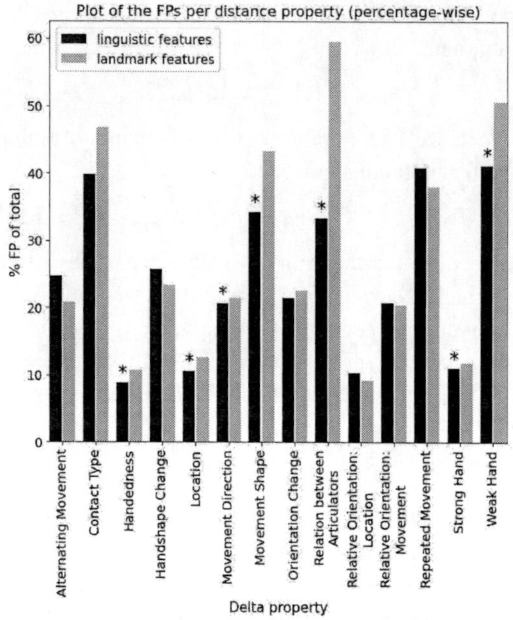

Figure 4: Percentage of confusable signs, per Δ property, that are falsely spotted ($*$=statistically sign. improvement)

property, are falsely spotted. We performed McNemar's test to analyze for which Δ properties there was a significant difference in performance between the models. An asterisk ($*$) is displayed where the difference is significant ($p < 0.05$).

For most Δ properties, the model trained using linguistic features outperforms the one trained with landmarks as it has a lower percentage of FP spottings. While there are some properties for which the model with landmark features produces fewer FP spottings, the difference is never found to be significant. For all Δ properties where we find a significant difference in performance, the linguistic feature model outperforms the landmark model. That said, it is evident that the linguistic feature model needs further improvement, since it still produces a substantial number of FP and FN predictions, and it does not significantly outperform the landmark model for some Δ properties.

5 Conclusion

In this paper, we investigated how linguistic features, extracted from landmarks of the hands and body of a signer, can be used in the context of sign spotting. We built on recent work in sign language recognition which derived an approximate representation of the handshape of a sign from Mediapipe landmarks, and developed our own features to capture the orientation, location and movement of the hands. We compared a sign spotting model

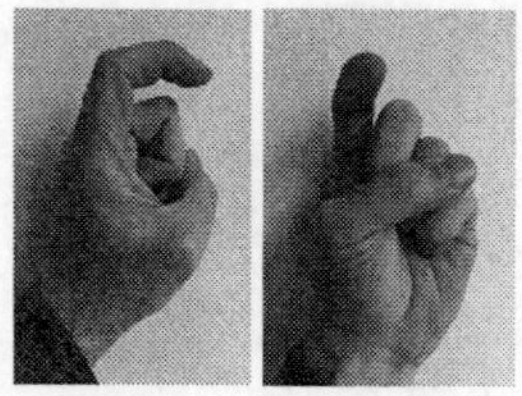

Figure 5: Hooked finger from two viewpoints

that uses these approximate linguistic features with a model that incorporates landmarks directly as training input. Our results show that the model using approximate linguistic features captures some aspects of signs better than the landmark model.

In future work, our approach to extracting linguistic features could be further improved. For example, the trajectory and repetition of movements may be better captured by including additional features besides wrist velocity. Furthermore, it could be interesting to train a model using a combination of landmark coordinates and linguistic features.

Our general approach will also benefit from further improved landmark detection technologies. Current technologies only reliably deliver 2D landmark coordinates. If an accurate estimation of the z coordinate were available, we could work with 3D representations of the hands and bodies of signers. Based on such 3D representations, linguistic features could be extracted in a more robust way. For instance, the left and right image in Figure 5 depict the same handshape viewed from two different angles. Based on 2D landmark coordinates, it would be possible to derive the curvature of the index finger under the perspective on the left (side view), but not under the perspective on the right (front view). From 3D landmark coordinates, the curvature could be derived precisely and reliably.

Another limitation of currently available landmark detection technologies, such as Mediapipe, is that they are not explicitly trained on sign language data. Certain handshapes are frequent in sign languages but may not be as frequent in general-purpose datasets. As a result, the current performance of Mediapipe and similar tools may be limited for such handshapes. That said, an important advantage of the modular approach we adopted is that it allows for the direct incorporation of future improvements of landmark detection technologies.

Finally, while not the focus of this work, we note that the model chosen to demonstrate the performance of the two types of features can be improved. A more sophisticated model architecture may result in better sign spotting performance.

References

Aljanaki, Anna, Frans Wiering, and Remco C Veltkamp. 2015. Emotion based segmentation of musical audio. In *Proceedings of the 16th conference of the international society for music information retrieval*, pages 770–776.

Battison, Robbin. 1978. *Lexical borrowing in American sign language*. Silver Spring, MD: Linstok Press.

Bowden, Richard, David Windridge, Timor Kadir, Andrew Zisserman, and Michael Brady. 2004. A linguistic feature vector for the visual interpretation of sign language. In *European conference on computer vision 2004: 8th european conference on computer vision*, pages 390–401. Springer.

Bragg, Danielle, Oscar Koller, Mary Bellard, Larwan Berke, Patrick Boudreault, Annelies Braffort, Naomi Caselli, Matt Huenerfauth, Hernisa Kacorri, Tessa Verhoef, Christian Vogler, and Meredith Ringel Morris. 2019. Sign language recognition, generation, and translation: An interdisciplinary perspective. In *The 21st association for computing machinery international special interest group on accessible computing conference on computers and accessibility*, pages 16–31.

Brentari, Diane, Jordan Fenlon, and Kearsy Cormier. 2018. Sign language phonology. In *Oxford research encyclopedia of linguistics*. Oxford University Press.

Brentari, Diane. 2019. *Sign Language Phonology*. Cambridge University Press.

Cao, Zhe, Tomas Simon, Shih-En Wei, and Yaser Sheikh. 2017. Realtime multi-person 2d pose estimation using part affinity fields. In *Proceedings of the IEEE conference on computer vision and pattern recognition*, pages 7291–7299.

Celebi, Sait, Ali Selman Aydin, Talha Tarik Temiz, and Tarik Arici. 2013. Gesture recognition using skeleton data with weighted dynamic time warping. *Proceedings of the international conference on computer vision theory and applications*, 1:620–625.

Chai, Junyi and Anming Li. 2019. Deep learning in natural language processing: A state-of-the-art survey. In *2019 International conference on machine learning and cybernetics*, pages 1–6. IEEE.

Cho, Seong-Sik, Hee-Deok Yang, and Seong-Whan Lee. 2009. Sign language spotting based on semi-markov conditional random field. In *2009 workshop on applications of computer vision*, pages 1–6. IEEE.

Crasborn, Onno and Inge Zwitserlood. 2008. The corpus NGT: an online corpus for professionals and laymen. *Construction and exploitation of sign language Corpora. 3rd workshop on the representation and processing of sign languages*, pages 44–49.

Crasborn, Onno, Inge Zwitserlood, and Johan Ros. 2008. The corpus NGT. an open access digital corpus of movies with annotations of sign language of the netherlands. *Centre for language Studies, Radboud University Nijmegen*.

Crasborn, Onno, Richard Bank, Inge Zwitserlood, Els van der Kooij, Anique SchÃ¼ller, Ellen Ormel, Ellen Nauta, Merel van Zuilen, Frouke van Winsum, and Johan Ros. 2014. NGT Signbank. *Centre for language Studies, Radboud University Nijmegen*.

Crasborn, Onno, Inge Zwitserlood, Els van der Kooij, and Anique Schüller. 2020. Global signbank manual. Technical report, version 2. Accessed on 5 April 2023.

Crasborn, Onno. 2012. Phonetics. In *Sign language: An international handbook*. De Gruyter.

De Vries, Arjen P, Gabriella Kazai, and Mounia Lalmas. 2004. Tolerance to irrelevance: A user-effort oriented evaluation of retrieval systems without predefined retrieval unit. In *RIAO conference proceedings*, pages 463–473.

Elmezain, Mahmoud, Ayoub Al-Hamadi, Jorg Appenrodt, and Bernd Michaelis. 2008. A hidden markov model-based continuous gesture recognition system for hand motion trajectory. In *2008 19th international conference on pattern recognition*, pages 1–4. IEEE.

Enrıquez, Manuel Vázquez, JL Alba-Castro, L Docio-Fernandez, JCSJ Junior, and S Escalera. 2022. Eccv 2022 sign spotting challenge: dataset, design and results. In *European conference on computer vision workshops*.

Farhan, Youssef and Abdessalam Ait Madi. 2022. Real-time dynamic sign recognition using mediapipe. In *2022 IEEE 3rd international conference on electronics, control, optimization and computer science*, pages 1–7. IEEE.

Han, Junwei, George Awad, and Alistair Sutherland. 2009. Modelling and segmenting subunits for sign language recognition based on hand motion analysis. *Pattern recognition letters*, 30(6):623–633.

He, Liwei, Elizabeth Sanocki, Anoop Gupta, and Jonathan Grudin. 1999. Auto-summarization of audio-video presentations. In *Proceedings of the seventh association for computing machinery international conference on multimedia (part 1)*, pages 489–498.

Hollain, Natalie, Martha Larson, and Floris Roelofsen. 2023. Distractor-based evaluation of sign spotting. *Sign language translation and avatar technology*.

Hussain, Muhammad Jamil, Ahmad Shaoor, Suliman A Alsuhibany, Yazeed Yasin Ghadi, Tamara al Shloul, Ahmad Jalal, and Jeongmin Park. 2022. Intelligent sign language recognition system for e-learning context. *Computers, materials & continua*, 72(3):5327–5343.

Jiang, Tao, Necati Cihan Camgöz, and Richard Bowden. 2021. Looking for the signs: Identifying isolated sign instances in continuous video footage. In *2021 16th IEEE international conference on automatic face and gesture recognition*, pages 1–8. IEEE.

Khosla, Prannay, Piotr Teterwak, Chen Wang, Aaron Sarna, Yonglong Tian, Phillip Isola, Aaron Maschinot, Ce Liu, and Dilip Krishnan. 2020. Supervised contrastive learning. *Advances in neural information processing systems*, 33:18661–18673.

Ko, Sang-Ki, Jae Gi Son, and Hyedong Jung. 2018. Sign language recognition with recurrent neural network using human keypoint detection. In *Proceedings of the 2018 conference on research in adaptive and convergent systems*, pages 326–328.

Ko, Sang-Ki, Chang Jo Kim, Hyedong Jung, and Choongsang Cho. 2019. Neural sign language translation based on human keypoint estimation. *Applied sciences*, 9(13):2683.

Momeni, Liliane, Gul Varol, Samuel Albanie, Triantafyllos Afouras, and Andrew Zisserman. 2020. Watch, read and lookup: learning to spot signs from multiple supervisors. In *Asian conference on computer vision*.

Moryossef, Amit and Yoav Goldberg. 2021. Sign Language Processing. https://sign-language-processing.github.io/. Accessed: Jan. 27, 2023.

Ong, Eng-Jon, Oscar Koller, Nicolas Pugeault, and Richard Bowden. 2014. Sign spotting using hierarchical sequential patterns with temporal intervals. In *Proceedings of the IEEE conference on computer vision and pattern recognition*, pages 1923–1930.

Pendzich, Nina-Kristin. 2020. *Lexical nonmanuals in German Sign Language: Empirical studies and theoretical implications*. De Gruyter.

Sandler, Wendy. 2012. The phonological organization of sign languages. *Language and linguistics compass*, 6(3):162–182.

Sengupta, Arindam, Feng Jin, Renyuan Zhang, and Siyang Cao. 2020. MM-Pose: Real-time human skeletal posture estimation using mmwave radars and cnns. *IEEE sensors journal*, 20(17):10032–10044.

Shin, Jungpil, Akitaka Matsuoka, Md Al Mehedi Hasan, and Azmain Yakin Srizon. 2021. American sign language alphabet recognition by extracting feature from hand pose estimation. *Sensors*, 21(17):5856.

Smith, Jordan BL and Elaine Chew. 2013. A meta-analysis of the mirex structure segmentation task. In *Proceedings of the 14th conference of the international society for music information retrieval*.

Smith, Jordan Bennett Louis, John Ashley Burgoyne, Ichiro Fujinaga, David De Roure, and J Stephen Downie. 2011. Design and creation of a large-scale database of structural annotations. In *Proceedings of the 12th international society for music information retrieval conference*, pages 555–560.

Stokoe, William. 1960. Sign language structure, an outline of the visual communications systems of american deaf. *Studies in linguistics occasional paper*, 8.

Tyrone, Martha. 2020. Phonetics of sign language. In *Oxford research encyclopedia of linguistics*. Oxford University Press.

Van der Kooij, Els. 2002. *Phonological categories in Sign Language of the Netherlands: The role of phonetic implementation and iconicity*. LOT.

Viitaniemi, Ville, Tommi Jantunen, Leena Savolainen, Matti Karppa, and Jorma Laaksonen. 2014. S-pot–a benchmark in spotting signs within continuous signing. In *Proceedings of the 9th international conference on language resources and evaluation*, pages 1892–1897. European Language Resources Association.

Von Agris, Ulrich, Jörg Zieren, Ulrich Canzler, Britta Bauer, and Karl-Friedrich Kraiss. 2008. Recent developments in visual sign language recognition. *Universal access in the information society*, 6:323–362.

Wong, Ryan, Necati Cihan Camgöz, and Richard Bowden. 2023. Hierarchical i3d for sign spotting. In *European conference on computer vision workshops*, pages 243–255. Springer.

Yang, Hee-Deok and Seong-Whan Lee. 2010. Simultaneous spotting of signs and fingerspellings based on hierarchical conditional random fields and boostmap embeddings. *Pattern recognition*, 43(8):2858–2870.

Zaki, Mahmoud M and Samir I Shaheen. 2011. Sign language recognition using a combination of new vision based features. *Pattern recognition letters*, 32(4):572–577.

Zhang, Fan, Valentin Bazarevsky, Andrey Vakunov, Andrei Tkachenka, George Sung, Chuo-Ling Chang, and Matthias Grundmann. 2020. Mediapipe hands: On-device real-time hand tracking. *arXiv preprint arXiv:2006.10214*.

A Linked Data Approach for linking and aligning Sign Language and Spoken Language Data

Thierry Declerck[1], **Sam Bigeard**[2], **Anas Fahad Khan**[3], **Irene Murtagh**[4], **Sussi Olsen**[5], **Michael Rosner**[6], **Ineke Schuurman**[7], **Andon Tchechmedjiev**[8], **Andy Way**[9]

[1]DFKI GmbH, Multilingual Technologies, Saarland Informatics Campus, D-66123 Saarbrücken, Germany
[2]Institute of German Sign Language and Communication of the Deaf University of Hamburg, Germany
[3]CNR-ILC, Italy
[4]Technological University Dublin, Ireland
[5]Centre for Language Technology, NorS, University of Copenhagen, Denmark
[6]Dept Artificial Intelligence, University of Malta
[7]Centre for Computational Linguistics, KU Leuven, 3000 Leuven, Belgium
[8]EuroMov-Digital Health in Motion, Univ. Montpellier, IMT Mines Alès, France
[9]ADAPT Centre, Dublin City University, Ireland

declerck@dfki.de, sam.bigeard@uni-hamburg.de, fahad.khan@ilc.cnr.it, irene.murtagh@adaptcentre.ie, saolsen@hum.ku.dk, mike.rosner@um.edu.mt, ineke.schuurman@ccl.kuleuven.be, andon.tchechmedjiev@mines-ales.fr, andy.way@adaptcentre.ie

Abstract

We present work dealing with a Linked Open Data (LOD)-compliant representation of Sign Language (SL) data, with the goal of supporting the cross-lingual alignment of SL data and their linking to Spoken Language (SpL) data. The proposed representation is based on activities of groups of researchers in the field of SL who have investigated the use of Open Multilingual Wordnet (OMW) datasets for (manually) cross-linking SL data or for linking SL and SpL data. Another group of researchers is proposing an XML encoding of articulatory elements of SLs and (manually) linking those to an SpL lexical resource. We propose an RDF-based representation of those various kinds of data. This unified formal representation offers a semantic repository of information on SL and SpL data that could be accessed for supporting the creation of datasets for training or evaluating NLP applications dealing with SLs, thinking for example of Machine Translation (MT) between SLs and between SLs and SpLs.

1 The Linguistic Linked Open Data Cloud and Sign Languages

Proponents of Linguistic Linked Open Data (LLOD) (Cimiano et al., 2020; Declerck et al., 2020) aim towards the representation of linguistic data through a standardised model based on the Resource Description Framework (RDF).[1] OntoLex-Lemon (Cimiano et al., 2016)[2] and its ecosystem (McCrae et al., 2017) are at the core of the LLOD cloud, and follow FAIR principles (Wilkinson et al., 2016)[3] to make linguistic data accessible and interoperable. This semantic interoperability allows for the interlinking of diverse linguistic datasets, establishing a well-connected subset of the Linked Open Data Cloud,[4] and creating avenues for analyses and studies long unattainable due to a history of barely interoperable formats. But the LLOD cloud does not currently include any Sign Language (SL) datasets, establishing the representation of SL data and Multimodality as a frontier for LLOD to accommodate.

[1]a W3C recommendation. See `https://www.w3.org/RDF/` for more details.
[2]See the following for the published specifications: `https://www.w3.org/2016/05/ontolex/`
[3]Where FAIR stands for Findable, Accessible, Interoperable and Reusable and refers to a series of well-known principles for ensuring that datasets can be described by each of the former adjectives.
[4]`http://cas.lod-cloud.net/clouds/linguistic-lod.svg`

D. Shterionov, M. De Sisto, M. Müller, D. Van Landuyt, R. Omardeen, S. Oboyle, A. Braffort, F. Roelofsen, F. Blain, B. Vanroy, E. Avramidis
Proceedings of the 2nd International Workshop on Automatic Translation for Signed and Spoken Languages, p. 13–23
Tampere, Finland, June 2023.

Declerck et al. (2023) discusses an RDF-based representation of the mapping between SL data and Spoken Language (SpL) resources via the Open Multilingual Wordnet (OMW) infrastructure, which is proposed in Bigeard et al. (2022). Elements of OntoLex-Lemon and cross-lingual linking techniques were used to create multilingual SL resources. Such work illustrates the potential to produce parallel training material at scale for MT between SLs or between SLs and SpLs.

These initial efforts have created momentum that has led to the explicit identification of SLs as a target for an extended representation within the OntoLex-Lemon model. This issue is also currently being discussed in the context of the BPMLOD W3C Community Group (detailed further in Section 3), which is producing a survey of existing best-practices to model linguistic (including SL) data as linked data.

One of the ways to ensure the interoperability of these heterogeneous resources, including across language types (SLs and SpLs), is through the use of FAIR principles for all aspects of the production/publication of the datasets (modelling, licensing, deposition in a repository, etc.).

We do not propose any new algorithms in this paper, but advocate for a standardised methodology for producing interoperable high-quality aligned datasets for SL and SpL (SSL) data using linked data and cross-lingual (within and across signed and spoken languages) technologies, as well as best practices and guidelines. For this, we need to involve various communities, and the W3C BPMLOD Community Group could offer a first forum for achieving our joint goals.

In the following, we first summarize the FAIR principles before introducing current, ongoing activities within the W3C BPMLOD Community Group. We then present four research initiatives dealing with the issue of SSL data alignments. For two of them, we already propose an RDF/OntoLex-Lemon modelization (Sections 4 and 5), while work is about to start for the SL data described in Sections 6 and 7.

2 FAIR Data and Linguistic Linked Open Data

FAIR data plays a central role in a number of prominent initiatives which have recently been proposed for the promotion of open science and data by numerous organisations and research funding bodies. We advocate that LLOD models can contribute to the creation of FAIR language resources.

It should come as no surprise, given the growing importance of open science initiatives and in particular those promoting the FAIR guidelines, that shared models and standardized vocabularies have begun to take on an increasingly prominent role within numerous disciplines, not least in the fields of linguistics and language resources. Although the linguistic linked data community has been active in advocating for the use of shared RDF-based vocabularies and models for quite some time now, this new emphasis on FAIR language resources is likely to have a considerable impact in several ways, in terms of the necessity for these models and vocabularies to demonstrate greater coverage with respect to the kinds of linguistic phenomena they can describe, and for them to be more interoperable with each other.

In *The FAIR Guiding Principles for scientific data management and stewardship* (Wilkinson et al., 2016), the article which first articulated the by-now ubiquitous FAIR principles, the authors state that the criteria proposed by those principles are intended both "for machines and people" and that they provide "'steps along a path' to machine actionability", where the latter is understood to describe structured data that would allow a "computational data explorer" to determine:

- the type of "digital research object";
- its usefulness with respect to tasks to be carried out;
- its usability especially with respect to licensing issues with this information represented in a way that would allow the agent to take "appropriate action".

The current popularity of the FAIR principles and, in particular, their promotion by governments, transnational organisations and research funding bodies, such as the European Commission,[5] reflects a wider recognition of the potential of structured, interoperable, machine-actionable data to help effect a major shift in how research is carried out, and in particular, its potential to help underpin open science best practices. The FAIR ideal,

[5] https://op.europa.eu/en/publication-detail/-/publication/7769a148-f1f6-11e8-9982-01aa75ed71a1/language-en/format-PDF/source-80611283

in short, is to allow machines (non-human software agents) a greater level of autonomy in working with data by rendering as much of the semantics of that data explicit (in the sense of machine-actionable) as possible.

Publishing data using a standardised, general purpose data model such as RDF[6] goes a long way towards facilitating the publication of datasets as FAIR data. RDF, taken together with the other standards proposed in the Semantic Web stack and the technical infrastructure which has been developed to support it, was specifically intended to facilitate interoperability and interlinking between datasets. In order to ensure the interoperability and reusability of datasets within a domain, however, it is vital that in addition to more generic data models such as RDF there also exist domain-specific vocabularies/terminologies/models and data category registries (compatible with the former). Such resources serve to describe, ideally in a machine-actionable way, the shared theoretical assumptions held by a community of domain experts as reflected in the terminology or terminologies in use within that community.

We note here that the emphasis placed on machine actionability in FAIR resources (that is, recall, on enabling computational agents to find relevant datasets and resources and to take "appropriate action" when they find them) gives Semantic Web vocabularies/models/registries a substantial advantage over other (non-Semantic Web-native) standards in the fields of linguistics and language resources. The OntoLex-Lemon ecosystem is to be understood in this light, aiming at enhancing the interoperability and machine actionability of linguistic datasets. It is, therefore, crucial to overcome the one limitation we noticed: there are for now no SL datasets within the LLOD, if we ignore the ongoing experiments in porting to RDF/OntoLex-Lemon the SL datasets (and their linking to OMW or other lexical resources) that are described in Sections 4, 5, 6, and 7.

3 The Best Practices for Multilingual Linked Open Data W3C Group

The BPMLOD W3C community group[7] initially created in 2015 to propose community-sourced guidelines for multilingual linked open data, has recently been resurrected in order to actualise the previously proposed guidelines, as there have been major evolutions in the field.

These renewed efforts have a much broader scope, covering topics such as neurosymbolic approaches to language processing, cross-lingual linking, multi-modality, and the representation of sign languages. The latter two specification efforts are central to establishing the foundational groundwork necessary for representing both SL and SpL data as RDF under the OntoLex family of models, as linked open data. The nature of semantic web technologies is conducive to easily enabling interlinking once both modalities can be represented in one harmonized formal model.

The BPMLOD Community Group has thus the potential of becoming a community nexus to channel work on semantic web models for SLs, SpLs and their linking. We encourage the widespread involvement of both the SL and the SpL communities in this initiative. As mentioned above, BPMLOD is currently working on a survey of existing best-practices to model linguistic (including SL) data as linked data.[8]

4 Aligning several SL Resources via the Open Multilingual WordNet Infrastructure

The work reported on in this section is developed within a research project, which aims to ease the communication between deaf and hearing individuals with the help of MT technologies. As such, linking different SLs through semantics is a priority. We chose to use the Open Multilingual Wordnet (OMW) infrastructure (Bond and Paik, 2012; Bond et al., 2016)[9] as a (semantic) pivot between SL data.

We are dealing with four languages (German, Greek, English and Dutch sign languages). The resources involved in our approach are the DGS corpus (Prillwitz et al., 2008), Noema+ GSL dictionary (Efthimiou et al., 2016), BSL signbank (Jordan et al., 2014), and the NGT global signbank (Crasborn et al., 2020). These resources contain various types of spoken language words associated with each sign. They may be keywords, equivalents, or SL glosses. They are used as a starting point to match with the lemmas present in

[6] https://www.w3.org/TR/rdf-primer/
[7] Best Practices for Multilingual Linked Open Data, see https://www.w3.org/community/bpmlod/
[8] The corresponding reports will be made available at https://github.com/bpmlod
[9] See also https://omwn.org/ for more details.

the corresponding (and aligned) language versions of OMW. Then, native signers manually validate the potential matches. By using the Open Multilingual Wordnet, we aim to identify the signs with the same (or related) senses across languages.

Each resource involved has different structures, and so, the method must be flexible enough to exploit all the data available and avoid mistakes. As an example, the DGS Corpus has a multi-level structure, where each sign can be a type, a sub-type, or a variant. Semantics are attached to the sub-type level. If a sense has been associated with a sub-type, it can be spread down to the variants associated with it, but not up to the type. The DGS Corpus also contains synonymy links that can be exploited to spread senses to other signs.

We describe in the following paragraphs elements of SLs that need to and could be (semantically) aligned across languages and language types.

Phonological transcriptions: While in an ideal world, those transcriptions from videos displaying signs could be used for establishing links between SL data for different languages, different SL data sets are transcribed with different transcription systems, e.g. HamNoSys (Hanke, 2004), SignWriting (Sutton, 1991) or others, as in the case of the Swedish SL data[10] or Irish SL, for which an XML-based transcription is under development (see Section 6 for more details).

Besides, even if two resources use the same transcription system, the level of accuracy or precision of the transcription is not the same for all data. In some cases the transcription can be either semi-automatically generated or produced by human transcribers with different skills and views on which phonological elements of a sign should be transcribed.[11]

We are aware of efforts being made toward analysing and processing the videos directly using machine learning, rather than comparing and aligning transcriptions, but those are not in the scope of our current work.

Glosses: Many projects dealing with SL use glosses to identify signs. A gloss is, typically, a spoken language word optionally followed by a sequence of numbers or letters, to allow several signs to share the same word. The word is typically related to the meaning or iconicity of the sign, in the surrounding SpL, for easier identification. But the used word is ultimately somewhat arbitrary. Two unrelated projects working on the same sign language might have different glosses for the same sign, or the same gloss for different signs. This creates an obstacle toward linking resources together.

While many SL resources use glosses for labelling their data, the low accuracy/precision of automated tagging and the low Inter-Annotator Agreement (IAA) between human annotators for such tagging made the glosses difficult to use as a potential cross-language instrument for interlinking SL data in various languages.[12]

For linking to the IDs in OMW, we preferably use keywords and translations as a starting point to approximate the meaning of the sign, and only use glosses as a last resort. However, we use glosses as identifiers.

5 Cross-Linking Nordic SL and SpL Data

We extended our RDF representation of the language coverage described in Section 4 to three Nordic languages: Danish, Icelandic and Swedish.

Troelsgård and Kristoffersen (2018) discuss approaches for ensuring consistency between (Danish) Sign Language corpus data and the Dictionary of Danish signs. This approach aims at delivering a correspondence between the dictionary lemmas and the corpus lexicon, which consists of types introduced for lemmatising the tokens found in the corpus annotations (glosses added to the signs). The strategy is to use words and their equivalents (also found in the dictionary) to search for signs in the corpus. In order to extend the list of potential Danish equivalents that could be used for a word-based search of signs in the corpus, Troelsgård and Kristoffersen (2018) suggest using the Danish wordnet, DanNet, which is described in Pedersen et al. (2009; Pedersen et al. (2018). This approach is thus very similar to the one described in Bigeard et al. (2022), but is 'limited' to the Danish language. The relations between sign identifiers and lexical elements from both DanNet and other dic-

[10] See (Bergman and Björkstrand, 2015) for a detailed description, and also `https://zrajm.github.io/teckentranskription/intro.html` on recent developments on a tool to support this transcription system.

[11] Power et al. (2022), for example, report in their experiment that the similarity (but not the exact matching) of transcriptions by two undergraduate research assistants working in a related project was 0.69.

[12] Forster et al. (2010) discuss, among others, best practices for gloss annotation, in order to mitigate the issues of divergent tagging results, even in one and the same corpus.

tionary sources are encoded in a database, from which we obtained a TSV export. Luckily for us, the wordnet elements encoded in this TSV export are the subset of DanNet entries that are contained in the Danish section of OMW.

In this export, we first have the signs, which correspond to entries in the Dictionary of Danish Signs (see Figure 1). A second type of data available in the export holds video links and information about the sign form (HamNoSys/SiGML). The HamNoSys notation, though, is rather coarse, as it is generated automatically from the dictionary's phonological descriptions, and it is not displayed at the web page. A third type of information included in the export concerns the senses associated with the signs and their (form) variants.

Our work consists thus in porting all those (interlinked) resources to RDF and OntoLex-Lemon, as we did for the data described in Section 4. In the OMW version of DanNet, we find for example the following information "00817680-n lemma beskyttelse", where the lemma corresponds to the OMW English wordnet "00817680-n lemma protection", thus sharing the same ID for the concept of "protection" in OMW (this holds also for French, etc.). We can therefore add the Danish sign ID (and video), which we obtained from the database, to our RDF-based infrastructure.

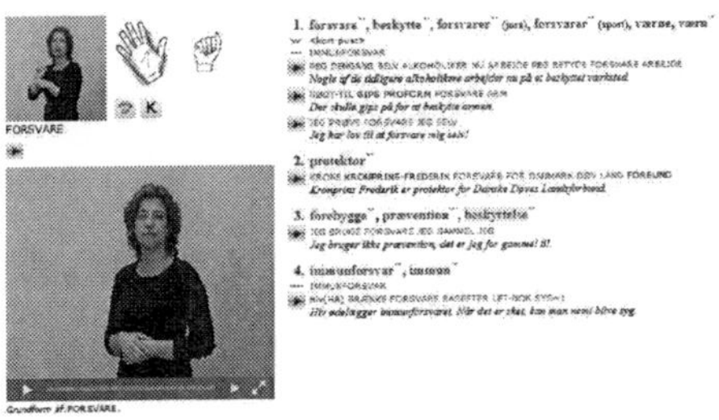

Figure 1: The Danish sign associated with the OMW ID "00817680-n", corresponding to the (highlighted) lemma "beskyttelse", here as one possible lexical realisation of the Danish gloss "FORSVARE" (*defend*)

Using the same strategy of deploying OMW as a pivot between concepts expressed in the videos, we extended our approach to Icelandic and Swedish. Through OMW we can find the lemmas for Icelandic and Swedish associated with the OMW IDs "1128193-v" and "00817680-n" (corresponding to the Danish lemmas). We use these to search in the Icelandic SignWiki,[13] and in the Swedish Sign Language Dictionary, described in Mesch et al. (2012).[14] Icelandic and Swedish glosses can be easily integrated in our RDF-based representation, as can be seen for example in Listing 1, where the gloss for the Danish sign depicted in Figure 1 is augmented with glosses or lemmas from other languages.

```
dts:GLOSS_dts-722
  rdf:type sl:GLOSS ;
  rdfs:label "\"FORSVARE\""@da ;
  rdfs:label "\"PROTEGER\""@fr ;
  rdfs:label "\"SCHUTZ1A^\""@de ;
  rdfs:label "\"protect(v)#1\""@en ;
  rdfs:label "\"beskydd\""@se ;
  rdfs:label "\"Vernda \""@is ;
.
```

Listing 1: The RDF-based representation of the gloss "FORSVARE", with the integration of multilingual labels from corresponding glosses

We further extended this approach to other Nordic languages, as described in Declerck and Olsen (2023).

6 A new Transcription System for the Irish Sign Language

Building on work dealing with linguistic properties of the Irish Sign Language (Murtagh, 2019), a group of researchers was confronted with the question of what is needed for creating an SL lexicon entry, as they wanted to document or "write down" what was being signed or articulated in the videos.

While SpL and SL share fundamental properties in relation to linguistic structure, certain modality-specific linguistic phenomena must be accommodated in computational terms, to allow for the modelling and processing of SLs. A new transcription system was developed for this, which, contrary to HamNoSys or SignWriting, is not based on iconic symbols, but directly encoded in XML.

The Sign_A framework (Murtagh et al., 2022) was developed with a view to providing a definition of linguistically motivated lexicon entries, that were sufficiently robust to accommodate sign language, in particular Irish Sign Language (ISL). Sign_A provides a formal description for the computational phonological parameters of SL. A Sign_A XML specification is provided for manual features (MFs), non-manual features (NMFs), location (both spatial and body anchored) information, and also temporal information. MFs include parameters for Hand ⟨HAND⟩, Handshape ⟨HS⟩, Hand Movement ⟨HM⟩, Palm Orientation

[13] https://is.signwiki.org/index.php/

[14] https://teckensprakslexikon.su.se

⟨PO⟩, Arm Movement ⟨AM⟩, Forearm ⟨FA⟩and Upper arm ⟨UA⟩. In Figure 2, we can see the Sign_A XML representation for the hands, where the "dominant hand" is defined as ⟨dh⟩, and the "non-dominant hand" as ⟨ndh⟩.

```
<MF>
    <HAND>
        <dh>"right"</dh>
        <ndh>"left"</ndh>
    </HAND>
    ...
</MF>
```

Figure 2: Initialising the right hand as the dominant hand

The NMFs include parameters for Eyebrow ⟨EB⟩, Eyelid ⟨EL⟩, Eye Gaze ⟨EG⟩, Cheek ⟨CHEEK⟩, Mouth ⟨MOUTH⟩, Tongue ⟨TNG⟩, Nose ⟨NOSE⟩, Shoulder ⟨SHOULDER⟩, Mouthing ⟨MOUTHING⟩, and Mouth Gesture ⟨MOUTHGESTURE⟩.

The head element ⟨HEAD⟩, contains a ⟨HEADMODE⟩ attribute, which can accept various actions pertaining to the head, e.g. nod, shake, tilt, turn, etc. We provide the XML specification for nodding the head twice in Figure 3.

```
<NMF>
    <HEAD>
        <HEADMODE>"nod"</HEADMODE>
        <TIMES>"2"</TIMES>
        ...
    </HEAD>
</NMF>
```

Figure 3: Specification for nodding the head twice

Sign_A also includes parameters to accommodate the location in space where a sign is articulated. The location parameters can be mapped to spatial locations ⟨LOC⟩ within the signing space and also to locations on the signer's body, referred to as body-anchored ⟨BA⟩ locations. Finally, the formalism also includes an XML specification for temporal information, where each phonological parameter has timing information associated with it, referred to as event duration ⟨ED⟩. Sign_A also includes a timeline parameter ⟨TL⟩, which refers to the overall timing of an utterance. This parameter is used to synchronise the simultaneous and parallel articulation of any given phonological parameter 'event' across an entire SL utterance.

While Sign_A offers a very detailed description (and a taxonomic structure) of articulatory elements of SLs, its XML encoding also eases the conversion of the data into RDF, a task we are starting on now. Another relevant aspect of the work pursued in the context of Sign_A is the attention given to linking the described sign to SpL lexical resources, as can be seen in Figure 4, which is taken from Murtagh et al. (2022).

Gloss	REAL LOVE MY JOB
English Translation	'I really love my job'
RRG+Sign_A Logical Structure	**LOVE'** <TEMPORAL><MF><NMF> (1sg, JOB)
ISL Lexicon XML SL Verb Entry	
<ISLGlossTranslate="LOVE" IPA="/lʌv/" LogicalStructure= "LOVE' <TEMPORAL> <LOCATION><MF><NMF> (1sg, JOB);" NumberVerb="sg" P.O.S="PlainVerb" personVerb="3rd" tenseVerb="PRES" love/>	
Lexeme Repository Sign_A XML description for Manual Features <MF> of SL verb LOVE	
<HAND><dh>"right"</dh><ndh>"left"</ndh></HAND>	
<HS><HSMode>unique</HSMode><HSID><value>24</value></HSID>	
<AM><Spatial><SOURCE>"locus'</SOURCE><GOAL>"locus'</GOAL>EDti></EDti><EDtn></EDtn> <TLti></TLti><TLtn></TLtn> </SPATIAL><AM>	
<PO><p2><p2_i><EDti></EDti><EDtn></EDtn></p2_i><p1_n><EDti></EDti><EDtn></EDtn></p2_n><TLti></TLti><TLtn></TLtn></p1></PO>	
Lexeme Repository Sign_A XML description for Non Manual Features <NMF> of SL verb LOVE	
<MOUTHING><VERB_ONE_TO_ONE><VERBIPA>"/lʌv/"</VERBIPA></VERB_ONE_TO_ONE></MOUTHING	

Figure 4: ISL plain verb "LOVE" lexeme repository and lexicon XML description.

Porting this cross-language type linking to RDF and OntoLex-Lemon will contribute to a full linking between SL and SpL lexical data, beyond the work described in Sections 4 and 5, which focus on the specific multilingual wordnet-based lexical resources for cross-linking SL data. We plan to link the Sign_A SL data to the DBnary resource (Sérasset and Tchechmedjiev, 2014; Sérasset, 2015) which represents lexical information extracted for 23 language editions available from Wiktionary in a way compliant with Linked Open Data.

7 SignNets - WordNets for a specific Type of Natural Language

In the Northern part of Belgium (Flanders), the official language is Dutch; in the Southern part (Wallonia), it is French. There are also two officially acknowledged sign languages, VGT (Flemish Sign Language) and LSFB (French Belgian Sign Language). Dutch is also the official spoken language in the Netherlands, but the officially acknowledged sign language is NGT (Dutch Sign Language). In this section, we concentrate on VGT and NGT, and the link with another natural language: spoken Dutch.[15] VGT and NGT are rather different SLs, having themselves developed quite independently. VGT tends to share characteristics with LSFB, even though they are growing apart. Nev-

[15]There are other sign languages which will have similar issues to solve, like ISL for which the surrounding spoken language is the variant of English used in Ireland. Another characteristic of ISL to be taken into account is that it is a gender-based SL, where men and women have different sign languages.

ertheless, similarities between VGT and NGT are noted especially when dealing with iconic signs, or when mouthing plays an important role, since in both cases the surrounding SpL is Dutch.

When linking via WordNet (OMW) it should be stressed that the glosses assigned to signs in fact represent a (semantic) concept instead of just words, i.e. they represent SpL synsets instead of a word belonging to such a synset. The gloss can even represent several parts of speech. Glosses used for specific concepts[16] may differ in NGT and VGT, but even the two providers of NGT data[17] may use different glosses for one and the same sign. In all these cases, even the part of speech of the chosen gloss may differ. [18]

In contrast, VGT and NGT may use the same gloss for different signs. Within VGT, one and the same gloss often represents a series of signs, all expressing the same concept. This is due to the regional variations of a sign, a property of VGT explicitly preserved by the Deaf Community after the official recognition of VGT. Note that especially older variants may disappear, while new ones pop up. In the Netherlands, the situation was the reverse: one sign per concept was pursued.[19] The VGT gloss will express the common concept. In both the NGT Signbank and the VGT dictionary, indicative translations in spoken Dutch are included to indicate the concept expressed. Quite often these represent several parts of speech like nouns and verbs, nouns and adjectives, etc.[20] We are linking these to the synsets per PoS included in OMW, but are also creating new, broader identifiers to link them to SL concepts, surpassing PoS differences.

In SignNet (Schuurman et al., to be published),[21] VGT thus comes with synsets of signs, whereas NGT usually does not. In SignNet signs (concepts) and words in spoken language are linked, using OMW, and adding hyponyms, hypernyms, homonyms, definitions of the concepts, etc.

There are at least two issues in doing so: first, OMW makes use of Open Dutch Wordnet, and ODW (and OMW) often use the Dutch meaning of a word, not the Flemish one. For example, 'voormiddag' refers to the hours before lunchtime in Flanders, and after lunch in the Netherlands. So we have to adapt ODW (and OMW) to cover such differences. We intend to do so by adding in ODW (and OMW) a 'geography' label "belg" to words that only are used in a specific sense in Flanders ('kleedje' instead of 'jurk' (dress)) or "ned" when the word is only used in the Netherlands ('kinderkopje' instead of 'kassei' (cobblestone)).

A second issue: quite often concepts labelled by one gloss in VGT (and NGT) cover more than one synset in the wordnet of the surrounding language, for example when several parts of speech are involved. However, sometimes also smaller sets are used: artists using voice taken together (singer, actor) vs artists not using voice (ballet dancer, painter, ...). Ebling et al. (2012) describe similar cases for the Swiss-German SL. And for example when the sign is rather iconic, showing a vertical versus a horizontal movement. In Dutch, there is the verb 'aanhaken' (hook on), used both to express hooking a painting on a hook in a wall (vertical) and hooking a trailer on a car (horizontal). In VGT and NGT, there are two different signs that respectively show a more vertically or horizontally oriented movement. Because this difference is not made in SpL, it is neither represented in ODW nor OMW, so we may need to adapt ODW in this respect as well.

Considerations of the similarities and differences between the two variants of the Dutch SLs and of the Dutch SpLs point to the need to properly address linguistic variations, if one wants to adequately interlink or align those variants across languages and language types. It seems that the current status of the OMW infrastructure cannot offer Wordnet IDs to serve as pivot in those cases. We thus need to address those issues in the next steps of our representation work in RDF, and to investigate whether the current "vartrans" module[22] of OntoLex-Lemon is adequately formulated for this

[16]Concept, not sign!

[17]Nederlands Gebarencentrum `https://www.gebarencentrum.nl` and the NGT part of the Global Signbank `https://signbank.cls.ru.nl/datasets/NGT`.

[18]In NGT the gloss for the concept covering 'arm' (poor) is BEHOEFTIG (an adjective), in VGT it is ARMOEDE (a noun).

[19]When in NGT more signs are covered using variants of the same gloss (BEHOEFTIG-A, BEHOEFTIG-B), quite often the coverage of the semantic concept differs. BEHOEFTIG-B can also mean 'broke', not only 'poor', which does not hold for BEHOEFTIG-A.

[20]Vossen (1999) refers to such words as being Near-Synonyms, referring to the EQ NEAR SYNONYM relation between 'aardig' (Adjective) in Dutch and 'to like' (verb) in English.

[21]Based on SL dictionaries, signbanks etc.

[22]See `https://www.w3.org/2016/05/ontolex/#variation-translation-vartrans` for more details.

task. An important lesson we can retain from this section is that the generation of parallel data for SL and SpL language variations is a challenging task.

8 A first Implementation of linking and aligning Strategies in RDF/OntoLex

Listing 1 has already shown how we can encode in RDF a Danish gloss and augment it with glosses or lemmas from other languages, which we extracted via the shared IDs implemented in OMW, pointing back to the Danish video equipped with the corresponding gloss. With the next Listings, we would like to give an idea of how the RDF and OntoLex-Lemon representation ensures the accurate linking of information in a standardized and interoperable way.

Listing 2 shows the encoding of the Danish video already displayed in Figure 1 above, and Listing 3 shows the RDF-based representation of the corresponding gloss.

```
<http://example.org/dts#
    SignVideos_dts-722.mp4>
 rdf:type sl:SignVideos ;
 sl:hasGLOSS dts:GLOSS_dts-722 ;
 sl:hasVideoAdresss "https://www.
     tegnsprog.dk/video/t/t_2162.mp4
     "^^rdf:HTML ;
 rdfs:label "\"Video annotated with
     the gloss 'FORSVARE'\""@en ;
.
```

Listing 2: The video annotated with the gloss "FORSVARE" as an instance of the RDF class "sl:SignVideos"

```
dts:GLOSS_dts-722
  rdf:type sl:GLOSS ;
  rdfs:label "\"FORSVARE\""@da ;
.
```

Listing 3: The RDF-based representation of the gloss "FORSVARE"

Listing 4 shows a corresponding lexical form (in this case a lemma taken from OMW) and links it to the video and to the gloss it is related to, also adding the SiGML notation, which is the XML transcription of the original HamNoSys code (Neves et al., 2020).

```
dts:Form_dts-722
  rdf:type ontolex:Form ;
  sl:hasGLOSS dts:GLOSS_dts-722 ;
  sl:hasVideo <http://example.org/dts#
      SignVideos_dts-722.mp4> ;
  sl:hasVideoAdresss "https://www.
      tegnsprog.dk/video/t/t_2162.mp4"^^
      rdf:HTML ;
  rdfs:label "\"Adding transcription
      information associated with the
      video with the gloss 'FORSVARE'\""
      @en ;
  ontolex:writtenRep "\"<sigml><hns_sign
      gloss='FORSVARE'><hamnosys_manual
      ><hamsymmlr/><hamfist/><hamparbegin
      /><hamextfingeru/><hampalmd/><
      hamplus/><hamextfingerr/><hampalmr
      /><hamparend/><hamparbegin/><
      hammoveu/><hamthumbside/><hamtouch
      /><hamplus/><hamnomotion/><
      hamparend/><hamrepeatfromstart/></
      hamnosys_manual></hns_sign></sigml
      >\"\""@hamnosys-sigml ;
  ontolex:writtenRep "\"beskyttelse\""
      @da ;
.
```

Listing 4: The RDF-based representation of the lexical form related to the gloss "FORSVARE" and the corresponding video

Finally, Listing 5 displays the lexical entry for which the form is a morphological realisation. The lexical entry is pointing to the OMW ID realised as a lexical concept in OntoLex-Lemon, and which itself points to the video annotated by the one gloss.

```
dts:LexicalEntry_722
  rdf:type ontolex:LexicalEntry ;
  rdfs:label "\"forsvare, beskytte,
      beskyttelse\""@da ;
  ontolex:evokes wnid:omw-00817680-n ;
  ontolex:lexicalForm dts:Form_722 ;
.
```

Listing 5: The RDF-based representation of the lexical entry, which relates the concept and the form

The full RDF code will be made available in a GitHub repository, so that interested colleagues can contribute to future developments.

9 Conclusion

We proposed in this paper to investigate the possibilities of a harmonised representation of data from both spoken and sign languages that were originally stored in different formats in different locations. Basing ourselves on the works and issues presented in Sections 4, 5, 6 and 7, we propose the use of RDF and associated standardized vocabularies or models (like OntoLex-Lemon) to support an interoperable encoding for constitutive elements of both SL and SpL resources and their interlinking and alignment, whilst also stressing the importance of following the principles of FAIR data.

We hope in this way to create a semantically organized repository of cross-lingual (both SLs and SpL) data, especially in the field of low-resource SLs, which can be of help for supporting the creation of data sets for training or evaluating NLP applications, thinking in the first place of automated translation.

Acknowledgements: Some of the work described is supported in part by the EASIER (Intelligent Automatic Sign Language Translation) Project. EASIER has received funding from the European Union's Horizon 2020 research and innovation programme, grant agreement n° 101016982. Other parts of the work described is carried out within the SignON (Sign Language Translation Mobile Application and Open Communications Frame) project. This project has received funding from the European Union's Horizon 2020 Research and Innovation Programme under Grant No. 101017255. Even other parts of the contribution to this work is supported by the LT-BRIDGE project, which has received funding from the European Union's Horizon 2020 Research and Innovation Programme under Grant Agreement No 952194. Contributions by many authors are done within the context of the COST Action NexusLinguarum – European network for Web-centred linguistic data science - (CA18209).

We would also like to thank the reviewers for their helpful comments on our submission.

References

[Bergman and Björkstrand2015] Bergman, Brita and Thomas Björkstrand. 2015. Teckentranskription. Technical Report XXV, Stockholm University, Sign Language.

[Bigeard et al.2022] Bigeard, Sam, Marc Schulder, Maria Kopf, Thomas Hanke, Kiki Vasilaki, Anna Vacalopoulou, Theodoros Goulas, Athanasia-Lida Dimou, Stavroula-Evita Fotinea, and Eleni Efthimiou. 2022. Introducing Sign Languages to a Multilingual Wordnet: Bootstrapping Corpora and Lexical Resources of Greek Sign Language and German Sign Language. In Efthimiou, Eleni, Stavroula-Evita Fotinea, Thomas Hanke, Julie A. Hochgesang, Jette Kristoffersen, Johanna Mesch, and Marc Schulder, editors, *Proceedings of the LREC2022 10th Workshop on the Representation and Processing of Sign Languages: Multilingual Sign Language Resources*, pages 9–15, Marseille, France, June. European Language Resources Association (ELRA).

[Bond and Paik2012] Bond, Francis and Kyonghee Paik. 2012. A Survey of WordNets and their Licenses. In *Proc. of the 6th Global WordNet Conference (GWC 2012)*, Matsue. 64–71.

[Bond et al.2016] Bond, Francis, Piek Vossen, John P. McCrae, and Christiane Fellbaum. 2016. Cili: the collaborative interlingual index. In *Proceedings of the Global WordNet Conference*, volume 2016.

[Cimiano et al.2016] Cimiano, Philipp, John McCrae, and Paul Buitelaar. 2016. Lexicon Model for Ontologies: Community Report, 10 May 2016. Technical report, W3C, May.

[Cimiano et al.2020] Cimiano, Philipp, Christian Chiarcos, John P. McCrae, and Jorge Gracia. 2020. *Linguistic Linked Data: Representation, Generation and Applications*. Springer International Publishing.

[Crasborn et al.2020] Crasborn, Onno, Richard Bank, Inge Zwitserlood, Els van der Kooij, Ellen Ormel, Johan Ros, Anique Schüller, Anne de Meijer, Merel van Zuilen, Yassine Ellen Nauta, Frouke van Winsum, and Max Vonk. 2020. Ngt dataset in global signbank.

[Declerck and Olsen2023] Declerck, Thierry and Sussi Olsen. 2023. Linked open data compliant representation of the interlinking of nordic wordnets and sign language data. In Ilinykh, Nikolai, Felix Morger, Dana Dannélls, Simon Dobnik, Beáta Megyesi, and Joakim Nivre, editors, *Proceedings of the 2nd Workshop on Resources and Representations for Under-Resourced Languages and Domains*, pages 62–69.

[Declerck et al.2020] Declerck, Thierry, John McCrae, Matthias Hartung, Jorge Gracia, Christian Chiarcos, Elena Montiel, Philipp Cimiano, Artem Revenko, Roser Sauri, Deirdre Lee, Stefania Racioppa, Jamal Nasir, Matthias Orlikowski, Marta Lanau-Coronas, Christian Fäth, Mariano Rico, Mohammad Fazleh Elahi, Maria Khvalchik, Meritxell Gonzalez, and Katharine Cooney. 2020. Recent developments for the linguistic linked open data infrastructure. In *Proceedings of the Twelfth International Conference on Language Resources and Evaluation (LREC 2020)*, pages 5660–5667. European Language Resources Association (ELRA).

[Declerck et al.2023] Declerck, Thierry, Thomas Troelsgård, and Sussi Olsen. 2023. Towards an rdf representation of the infrastructure consisting in using wordnets as a conceptual interlingua between multilingual sign language datasets. In *GWC 2023: 12th International Global Wordnet Conference, Proceedings*, 01. to appear.

[Ebling et al.2012] Ebling, Sarah, Katja Tissi, and Martin Volk. 2012. Semi-Automatic Annotation of Semantic Relations in a Swiss German Sign Language Lexicon. In Crasborn, Onno, Eleni Efthimiou, Stavroula-Evita Fotinea, Thomas Hanke, Jette Kristoffersen, and Johanna Mesch, editors, *Proceedings of the LREC2012 5th Workshop on the Representation and Processing of Sign Languages: Interactions between Corpus and Lexicon*, pages 31–36, Istanbul, Turkey, May. European Language Resources Association (ELRA).

[Efthimiou et al.2016] Efthimiou, Eleni, Stavroula-Evita Fotinea, Thomas Hanke, Julie A. Hochgesang, Jette Kristoffersen, and Johanna Mesch, editors. 2016. *Proceedings of the LREC2016 7th Workshop on the Representation and Processing of Sign*

Languages: Corpus Mining, Portorož, Slovenia, May. European Language Resources Association (ELRA).

[Forster et al.2010] Forster, Jens, Daniel Stein, Ellen Ormel, Onno Crasborn, and Hermann Ney. 2010. Best practice for sign language data collections regarding the needs of data-driven recognition and translation. In *Proceedings of the 4th Workshop on the Representation and Processing of Sign Languages: Corpora and Sign Language Technologies (CSLT 2010)*, 01.

[Hanke2004] Hanke, Thomas. 2004. HamNoSys – representing sign language data in language resources and language processing contexts. In Streiter, Oliver and Chiara Vettori, editors, *Proceedings of the LREC2004 Workshop on the Representation and Processing of Sign Languages: From SignWriting to Image Processing. Information techniques and their implications for teaching, documentation and communication*, pages 1–6, Lisbon, Portugal, May. European Language Resources Association (ELRA).

[Jordan et al.2014] Jordan, Fenlon, Kearsy Cormier, Ramas Rentelis, Adam Schembri, Katherine Rowley, Robert Adam, and Bencie Woll. 2014. Bsl signbank: A lexical database of british sign language (first edition).

[McCrae et al.2017] McCrae, John P, Julia Bosque-Gil, Jorge Gracia, Paul Buitelaar, and Philipp Cimiano. 2017. The OntoLex-Lemon Model: Development and Applications. In *Electronic lexicography in the 21st century. Proceedings of eLex 2017*, pages 587–597. Lexical Computing CZ s.r.o.

[Mesch et al.2012] Mesch, Johanna, Lars Wallin, and Thomas Björkstrand. 2012. Sign language resources in Sweden: Dictionary and corpus. In Crasborn, Onno, Eleni Efthimiou, Stavroula-Evita Fotinea, Thomas Hanke, Jette Kristoffersen, and Johanna Mesch, editors, *Proceedings of the LREC2012 5th Workshop on the Representation and Processing of Sign Languages: Interactions between Corpus and Lexicon*, pages 127–130, Istanbul, Turkey, May. European Language Resources Association (ELRA).

[Murtagh et al.2022] Murtagh, Irene, Víctor Ubieto Nogales, and Josep Blat. 2022. Sign language machine translation and the sign language lexicon: A linguistically informed approach. In *Proceedings of the 15th biennial conference of the Association for Machine Translation in the Americas (Volume 1: Research Track)*, pages 240–251, Orlando, USA, September. Association for Machine Translation in the Americas.

[Murtagh2019] Murtagh, Irene. 2019. *A Linguistically Motivated Computational Framework for Irish Sign Language*. Ph.D. thesis, Trinity College Dublin.

[Neves et al.2020] Neves, Carolina, Luísa Coheur, and Hugo Nicolau. 2020. HamNoSyS2SiGML: Translating HamNoSys into SiGML. In *Proceedings of the 12th Language Resources and Evaluation Conference*, pages 6035–6039, Marseille, France, May. European Language Resources Association.

[Pedersen et al.2009] Pedersen, Bolette Sandford, Sanni Nimb, Jørg Asmussen, Nicolai Hartvig Sørensen, Lars Trap-Jensen, and Henrik Lorentzen. 2009. DanNet — the challenge of compiling a wordnet for Danish by reusing a monolingual dictionary. *Language Resources and Evaluation*, 43(3):269–299.

[Pedersen et al.2018] Pedersen, Bolette Sandford, Manex Aguirrezabal Zabaleta, Sanni Nimb, Sussi Olsen, and Ida Rørmann Olsen. 2018. Towards a principled approach to sense clustering – a case study of wordnet and dictionary senses in danish. In *Proceedings of Global WordNet Conference 2018*. Global WordNet Association. null ; Conference date: 08-01-2018 Through 12-01-2018.

[Power et al.2022] Power, Justin, David Quinto-Pozos, and Danny Law. 2022. Signed language transcription and the creation of a cross-linguistic comparative database. In *Proceedings of the LREC2022 10th Workshop on the Representation and Processing of Sign Languages: Multilingual Sign Language Resources*, pages 173–180, Marseille, France, June. European Language Resources Association.

[Prillwitz et al.2008] Prillwitz, Siegmund, Thomas Hanke, Susanne König, Reiner Konrad, Gabriele Langer, and Arvid Schwarz. 2008. DGS Corpus project – development of a corpus based electronic dictionary German Sign Language / German. In Crasborn, Onno, Eleni Efthimiou, Thomas Hanke, Ernst D. Thoutenhoofd, and Inge Zwitserlood, editors, *Proceedings of the LREC2008 3rd Workshop on the Representation and Processing of Sign Languages: Construction and Exploitation of Sign Language Corpora*, pages 159–164, Marrakech, Morocco, June. European Language Resources Association (ELRA).

[Schuurman et al.to be published] Schuurman, Ineke, Thierry Declerck, Caro Brosens, Margot Jassens, Vincent Vandeghinste, and Bram Vanroy. to be published. Are there just WordNets or also SignNets? In *Proceedings of the 13th Global WordNet Conference*.

[Sérasset2015] Sérasset, Gilles. 2015. DBnary: Wiktionary as a Lemon-based multilingual lexical resource in RDF. *Semantic Web*, 6(4):355–361. Publisher: IOS Press.

[Sutton1991] Sutton, V. 1991. *Lessons in Sign Writing: Textbook*. Cent. for Sutton Movement Writ.

[Sérasset and Tchechmedjiev2014] Sérasset, Gilles and Andon Tchechmedjiev. 2014. Dbnary : Wiktionary as Linked Data for 12 Language Editions with Enhanced Translation Relations. In *3rd Workshop on Linked Data in Linguistics: Multilingual Knowledge Resources and Natural Language Processing*, page to appear, Reyjkjavik, France.

[Troelsgård and Kristoffersen2018] Troelsgård, Thomas and Jette Kristoffersen. 2018. Improving lemmatisation consistency without a phonological description. the Danish Sign Language corpus and dictionary project. In Bono, Mayumi, Eleni Efthimiou, Stavroula-Evita Fotinea, Thomas Hanke, Julie A. Hochgesang, Jette Kristoffersen, Johanna Mesch, and Yutaka Osugi, editors, *Proceedings of the LREC2018 8th Workshop on the Representation and Processing of Sign Languages: Involving the Language Community*, pages 195–198, Miyazaki, Japan, May. European Language Resources Association (ELRA).

[Vossen1999] Vossen, Piek. 1999. EuroWordNet General Document. Technical report, University of Amsterdam, The Netherlands.

[Wilkinson et al.2016] Wilkinson, Mark D., Michel Dumontier, IJsbrand Jan Aalbersberg, Gabrielle Appleton, Myles Axton, Arie Baak, Niklas Blomberg, Jan-Willem Boiten, Luiz Bonino da Silva Santos, Philip E. Bourne, Jildau Bouwman, Anthony J. Brookes, Tim Clark, Mercè Crosas, Ingrid Dillo, Olivier Dumon, Scott Edmunds, Chris T. Evelo, Richard Finkers, Alejandra Gonzalez-Beltran, Alasdair J. G. Gray, Paul Groth, Carole Goble, Jeffrey S. Grethe, Jaap Heringa, Peter A. C. 't Hoen, Rob Hooft, Tobias Kuhn, Ruben Kok, Joost Kok, Scott J. Lusher, Maryann E. Martone, Albert Mons, Abel L. Packer, Bengt Persson, Philippe Rocca-Serra, Marco Roos, Rene van Schaik, Susanna-Assunta Sansone, Erik Schultes, Thierry Sengstag, Ted Slater, George Strawn, Morris A. Swertz, Mark Thompson, Johan van der Lei, Erik van Mulligen, Jan Velterop, Andra Waagmeester, Peter Wittenburg, Katherine Wolstencroft, Jun Zhao, and Barend Mons. 2016. The FAIR Guiding Principles for scientific data management and stewardship. *Scientific Data*, 3(1):160018, March.

An Open-Source Gloss-Based Baseline for Spoken to Signed Language Translation

Amit Moryossef[1,2], Mathias Müller[2], Anne Göhring[2], Zifan Jiang[2], Yoav Goldberg[1], Sarah Ebling[2]
[1]Bar-Ilan University, [2]University of Zurich
amitmoryossef@gmail.com

https://github.com/ZurichNLP/spoken-to-signed-translation

Abstract

Sign language translation systems are complex and require many components. As a result, it is very hard to compare methods across publications. We present an open-source implementation of a text-to-gloss-to-pose-to-video pipeline approach, demonstrating conversion from German to Swiss German Sign Language, French to French Sign Language of Switzerland, and Italian to Italian Sign Language of Switzerland. We propose three different components for the text-to-gloss translation: a lemmatizer, a rule-based word reordering and dropping component, and a neural machine translation system. Gloss-to-pose conversion occurs using data from a lexicon for three different signed languages, with skeletal poses extracted from videos. To generate a sentence, the text-to-gloss system is first run, and the pose representations of the resulting signs are stitched together.

1 Introduction

Sign language plays a crucial role in communication for many deaf[1] individuals worldwide. However, producing sign language content is often a challenging, laborious, and time-consuming process, requiring skilled translators/interpreters for effective communication. Recent technological advancements have led to the development of automated sign language translation systems, which have the potential to increase accessibility for the deaf community and enhance communication.

One of the critical issues in this field is the lack of a reproducible and reliable baseline for sign language translation systems. Without a baseline, it is challenging to measure the progress and effectiveness of new methods and systems. Additionally, the absence of such a baseline makes it difficult for new researchers to enter the field, hampers comparative evaluation, and discourages innovation.

Addressing this gap, this paper presents an open-source implementation of a text-to-gloss-to-pose-to-video pipeline approach for sign language translation, extending the work of Stoll et al. (2018; 2020). Our main contribution is the development of an open-source, reproducible baseline that can aid in making sign language translation systems more available and accessible, particularly in resource-limited settings. This open-source approach allows the community to identify issues, work together on improving these systems, and facilitates research into novel techniques and strategies for sign language translation

Our approach involves three alternatives for text-to-gloss translation, including a lemmatizer, a rule-based word reordering and dropping component, and a neural machine translation (NMT) system. For gloss-to-pose conversion, we use lexicon-acquired data for three signed languages, including Swiss German Sign Language (DSGS), Swiss French Sign Language (LSF-CH), and Swiss Italian Sign Language (LIS-CH). We extract skeletal poses using a state-of-the-art pose estimation framework, and apply a series of improvements to the poses, including cropping, concatenation, and smoothing, before applying a smoothing filter.

[1]We follow the recent convention of abandoning a distinction between "Deaf" and "deaf", using the latter term also to refer to (deaf) members of the sign language community (Kusters et al., 2017; Napier and Leeson, 2016).

D. Shterionov, M. De Sisto, M. Müller, D. Van Landuyt, R. Omardeen, S. Oboyle, A. Braffort, F. Roelofsen, F. Blain, B. Vanroy, E. Avramidis
Proceedings of the 2nd International Workshop on Automatic Translation for Signed and Spoken Languages, p. 25–36
Tampere, Finland, June 2023.

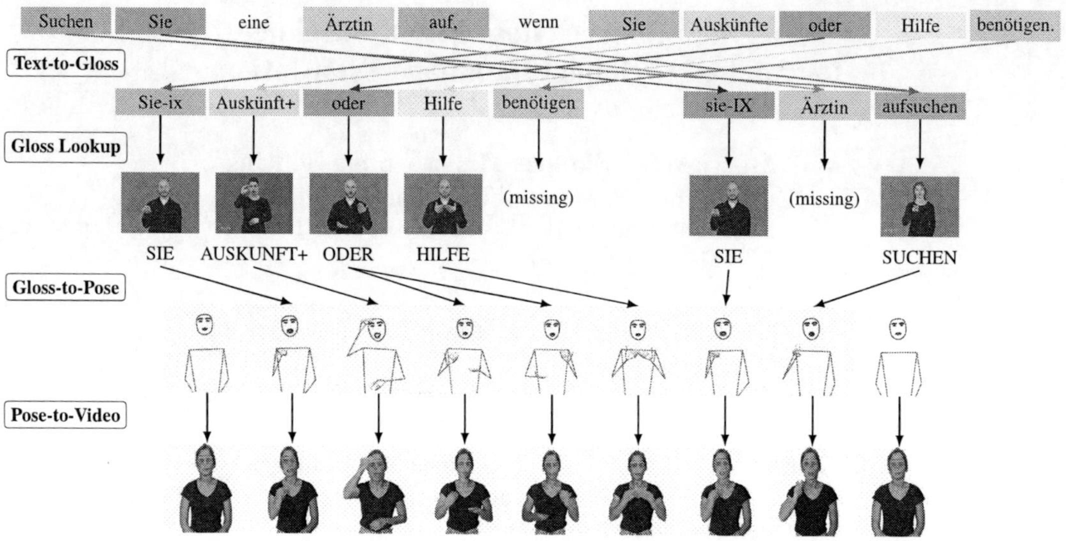

Figure 1: The figure depicts the entire pipeline of the proposed text-to-gloss-to-pose-to-video approach for sign language translation. Starting with a German sentence, the system applies text-to-gloss translation, for example, using a rule-based word reordering and dropping component. The resulting gloss sequence is used to search for relevant videos from a lexicon of Swiss German Sign Language (DSGS). The poses of each relevant video are then extracted and concatenated in the gloss-to-pose step to create a pose sequence for the sentence, which is then transformed back to a (synthesized) video using the pose-to-video model. The figure demonstrates the transformation of the sentence "Suchen Sie eine Ärztin auf, wenn Sie Auskünfte oder Hilfe benötigen." ('Seek out a doctor if you need information or assistance.') to a sequence of glosses, the search for relevant videos for each gloss, the concatenation of pose videos, and the final video output.

2 Background

Sign language translation can be accomplished in various ways. In this section, we focus on the pipeline approach that involves text-to-gloss, gloss-to-pose, and, optionally, pose-to-video techniques. The text-to-gloss technique translates spoken language text into sign language glosses, which are then converted into a sequence of poses by gloss-to-pose techniques, and into a photorealistic video using pose-to-video techniques.

This pipeline offers the benefit of preserving the content of the sentence, while exhibiting a tendency for verbosity and a lower degree of fluency. In this section, we explore each of the pipeline components comprehensively and examine recent progress in sign language translation utilizing these methods.

2.1 Text-to-Gloss

Text-to-gloss, an instantiation of sign language translation, is the task of translating between a spoken language text and sign language glosses. It is an appealing area of research because of its simplicity for integrating in existing NMT pipelines, despite recent works such as Yin and Read (2020) and Müller et al. (2022) claim that glosses are an inefficient representation of sign language, and that glosses are not a complete representation of signs (Pizzuto et al., 2006).

Zhao et al. (2000) used a Tree Adjoining Grammar (TAG)-based system to translate English sentences to American Sign Language (ASL) gloss sequences. They parsed the English text and simultaneously assembled an ASL gloss tree, using Synchronous TAGs (Shieber and Schabes, 1990; Shieber, 1994), by associating the ASL elementary trees with the English elementary trees and associating the nodes at which subsequent substitutions or adjunctions can occur. Synchronous TAGs have been used for machine translation between spoken languages (Abeillé et al., 1991), but this was the first application to a signed language.

Othman and Jemni (2012) identified the need for a large parallel sign language gloss and spoken language text corpus. They developed a part-of-speech-based grammar to transform English sentences from the Gutenberg Project ebooks collection (Lebert, 2008) into American Sign Language gloss. Their final corpus contains over 100 million synthetic sentences and 800 million words and is the most extensive English-ASL gloss corpus we know of. Unfortunately, it is hard to attest to the quality of the corpus, as the authors did not evaluate their method on real English-ASL gloss pairs.

Egea Gómez et al. (2021) presented a syntax-aware transformer for this task, by injecting word dependency tags to augment the embeddings inputted to the encoder. This involves minor modifications in the neural architecture leading to negligible impact on computational complexity of the model. Testing their model on the RWTH-PHOENIX-Weather-2014T (Camgöz et al., 2018), they demonstrated that injecting this additional information results in better translation quality.

2.2 Gloss-to-Pose

Gloss-to-pose, subsumed under the task of sign language production, is the task of producing a sequence of poses that adequately represent a sequence of signs written as gloss.

To produce a sign language video, Stoll et al. (2018) construct a lookup table between glosses and sequences of 2D poses. They align all pose sequences at the neck joint of a reference skeleton and group all sequences belonging to the same gloss. Then, for each group, they apply dynamic time warping and average out all sequences in the group to construct the mean pose sequence. This approach suffers from not having an accurate set of poses aligned to the gloss and from unnatural motion transitions between glosses.

To alleviate the downsides of the previous work, Stoll et al. (2020) construct a lookup table of gloss to a group of sequences of poses rather than creating a mean pose sequence. They build a Motion Graph (Min and Chai, 2012), which is a Markov process used to generate new motion sequences that are representative of natural motion, and select the motion primitives (sequence of poses) per gloss with the highest transition probability. To smooth that sequence and reduce unnatural motion, they use a Savitzky–Golay motion transition smoothing filter (Savitzky and Golay, 1964).

2.3 Pose-to-Video

Pose-to-video, also known as motion transfer or skeletal animation in the field of robotics and animation, is the conversion of a sequence of poses to a video. This task is the final "rendering" of sign language in a visual modality.

Chan et al. (2019) demonstrated a semi-supervised approach where they took a set of videos, ran pose estimation with OpenPose (Cao et al., 2019), and learned an image-to-image translation (Isola et al., 2017) between the rendered skeleton and the original video. They demonstrated their approach on human dancing, where they could extract poses from a choreography and render any person as if *they* were dancing. They predicted two consecutive frames for temporally coherent video results and introduced a separate pipeline for a more realistic face synthesis, although still flawed.

Wang et al. (2018) suggested a similar method using DensePose (Güler et al., 2018) representations in addition to the OpenPose (Cao et al., 2019) ones. They formalized a different model, with various objectives to optimize for, such as background-foreground separation and temporal coherence by using the previous two timestamps in the input.

Using the method of Chan et al. (2019) on "Everybody Dance Now", Ventura et al. (2020) asked, "Can Everybody Sign Now?" and investigated if people could understand sign language from automatically generated videos. They conducted a study in which participants watched three types of videos: the original signing videos, videos showing only poses (skeletons), and reconstructed videos with realistic signing. The researchers evaluated the participants' understanding after watching each type of video. The results of the study revealed that participants preferred the reconstructed videos over the skeleton videos. However, the standard video synthesis methods used in the study were not effective enough for clear sign language translation. Participants had trouble understanding the reconstructed videos, suggesting that improvements are needed for better sign language translation in the future.

As a direct response, Saunders et al. (2020) showed that like in Chan et al. (2019), where an adversarial loss was added to specifically generate the face, adding a similar loss to the hand generation process yielded high-resolution, more photo-realistic continuous sign language videos. To further improve the hand image synthesis quality, they introduced a keypoint-based loss function to avoid issues caused by motion blur.

In a follow-up paper, Saunders et al. (2021) introduced the task of Sign Language Video Anonymisation (SLVA) as an automatic method to anonymize the visual appearance of a sign language video while retaining the original sign language content. Using a conditional variational autoencoder framework, they first extracted pose information from the source video to remove the original signer appearance, then generated a photo-realistic sign language video of a novel appearance from the pose sequence. The authors proposed a novel style loss that ensures style consistency in the anonymized sign language videos.

3 Method

In this section, we provide an overview of our text-to-gloss-to-pose-to-video pipeline, detailing the components and how they work together to convert input spoken language text into a sign language video. The pipeline consists of three main components: text-to-gloss translation, gloss-to-pose conversion, and pose-to-video animation. For text-to-gloss translation, we provide three different alternatives: a lemmatizer, a rule-based word reordering and dropping component, and a neural machine translation system. Figure 1 illustrates the entire pipeline and its components.

3.1 Pipeline

Below, we describe the high-level structure of our pipeline, including the text-to-gloss translation, gloss-to-pose conversion, and pose-to-video animation components:

1. **Text-to-Gloss Translation:** The input (spoken language) text is first processed by the text-to-gloss translation component, which converts it into a sequence of glosses.

2. **Gloss-to-Pose Conversion:** The sequence of glosses generated from the previous step is then used to search for relevant videos from a lexicon of signed languages (e.g., DSGS, LSF-CH, LIS-CH). We extract the skeletal poses from the relevant videos using a state-of-the-art pre-trained pose estimation framework. These poses are then cropped, concatenated, and smoothed, creating a pose representation for the input sentence.

3. **Pose-to-Video Generation:** The processed pose video is transformed back into a synthesized video using an image translation model, based on a custom training of Pix2Pix.

3.2 Implementation Details

Our system accepts spoken language text as input and outputs an *.mp4* video file, or a binary *.pose* file, which can be handled by the *pose-format* library (Moryossef and Müller, 2021) in Python and JavaScript. The *.pose* file represents the sign language pose sequence generated from the input text. To make our system easy to use, we deploy it as an HTTP endpoint that receives text as input and outputs the *.pose* file. We provide a demonstration of our system using `https://sign.mt`, with support for the three signed languages of Switzerland.

We implement our pipeline using Python and package it using Flask, a lightweight web framework. This allows us to create an HTTP endpoint for our application, making it easy to integrate with other systems and web applications. Our system is deployed on a Google Cloud Platform (GCP) server, providing scalability and easy access. Furthermore, we release the source code of our implementation as open-source software, allowing others to build upon our work and contribute to improving the accessibility of sign language translation systems.

By implementing our system as an open-source Python application and deploying it as an HTTP endpoint, we aim to facilitate collaboration and improvements to sign language translation systems.

4 Text-to-Gloss

We explore three different components as part of text-to-gloss translation, including a lemmatizer (§4.1), a rule-based word reordering and dropping component (§4.2), and a neural machine translation (NMT) system (§4.3).

4.1 Lemmatizer

We use the *Simplemma* simple multilingual lemmatizer for Python (Barbaresi, 2023). The lemmatizer reduces words to their base form (i.e., lemma), which is useful for our case, as it helps to preserve meaning while reducing the complexity of the input. This approach is limited by the use of the simplistic context-free lemmatizer, since no sense information is captured in the lemma, which causes ambiguity.

4.2 Word Reordering and Dropping

We generate near-glosses for sign language from spoken language text using a rule-based approach. The process from converting spoken language sentences into sign language gloss sequences can be naively summarized by a removal of word inflection, an omission of punctuation and specific words, and word reordering. To address these differences, we adopt the rule-based approach from

Moryossef et al. (2021) to generate near-glosses from spoken language: lemmatization of spoken words, PoS-dependent word deletion, and word order permutation. With their permission, we re-share these rules:

Specifically, we use spaCy (Montani et al., 2023) for lemmatization, PoS tagging and dependency parsing. Unlike Simplelemma, the spaCy lemmatizer is language specific and context based. We drop words that are not content words (e.g., articles, prepositions), as they are largely unused in signed languages, but keep possessive and personal pronouns as well as nouns, verbs, adjectives, adverbs, and numerals. We devise a short list of syntax transformation rules based on the grammar of the sign language and the corresponding spoken language. We identify the subject, verb, and object in the input text and reorder them to match the order used in the signed language. For example, for German-to-German Sign Language (*Deutsche Gebärdensprache*, DGS), we reorder SVO sentences to SOV, move verb modifying adverbs and location words to the start of the sentence (a form of topicalization), move negation words to the end.

The specific rules we use for German to DGS/DSGS are:

1. For each subject-verb-object triplet $(s, v, o) \in \mathcal{S}$, swap the positions of v and o in $\mathcal{S}$
2. Keep all tokens $t \in \mathcal{S}$ if $\mathbf{PoS}(t) \in \{$noun, verb, adjective, adverb, numeral, pronoun$\}$
3. If $\mathbf{PoS}(t)$ = adverb and $\mathbf{HEAD}(t)$ = verb, move t to the start of S
4. If $\mathbf{NER}(t)$ = location, move t to the start of S
5. If $\mathbf{DEP}(t)$ = negation, move t to the end of S
6. Lemmatize all tokens $t \in \mathcal{S}$

We first split each sentence into separate clauses and reorder them before we apply these rules to each clause. Reordering the clauses may be needed for conditional sentences where the conditional subordinate clause should precede the main clause, as in "if...then...". These rules allow us to transform spoken language text into near-glosses that more closely match the word order and structure of sign language. Overall, our rule-based approach provides a flexible and effective way to generate near-glosses for sign language from spoken language text, with the ability to incorporate language-specific rules to capture the nuances of different sign languages. This approach employs a more accurate lemmatizer, however, it still suffers from word sense ambiguity.

4.3 Neural Machine Translation

As an alternative to rule-based transformations of text to glosses, we train a neural machine translation (NMT) system.

Data We use the Public DGS Corpus, a publicly available corpus of German Sign Language videos with annotated glosses (Hanke et al., 2020). Appendix B explains our data loading and preprocessing in more detail. We hold out a random sample of 1k training examples each for development and testing purposes. Table 1 shows an overview of the number of sentence pairs in all splits.

Partition	**Available Languages**			
	EN	**DGS·DE**	**DGS·EN**	**DE**
Train	61912	61912	61912	61912
Dev	1000	1000	1000	1000
Test	1000	1000	1000	1000
Total	**63912**	**63912**	**63912**	**63912**

Table 1: Number of sentence pairs used for gloss models. DGS·DE=original gloss transcriptions, DGS·EN=DGS glosses translated to English.

Preprocessing Our preprocessing and model settings are inspired by OPUS-MT (Tiedemann and Thottingal, 2020). The only preprocessing step that we apply to all data is Sentencepiece segmentation (Kudo, 2018). We learn a shared vocabulary with a desired total size of 1k pieces.

We additionally preprocess DGS glosses in a corpus-specific way, informed by the DGS Corpus glossing conventions (Konrad et al., 2022). The exact steps are given in Appendix B.1. See Table 2 for examples for this preprocessing step. Overall the desired effect is to reduce the number of observed forms while not altering the meaning itself.

Core model settings We train NMT models with Sockeye 3 (Hieber et al., 2022). The models are standard Transformer models (Vaswani et al., 2017), except with some hyperparameters modified for a low-resource scenario. E.g., dropout rate is set to a high value of 0.5 for all dropout layers of the model (Sennrich and Zhang, 2019).

The NMT system itself is trained with three-way weight tying between the source embeddings, target embeddings matrix and softmax output (Press and Wolf, 2017).

We train a multilingual model, following the methodology described in Johnson et al. (2017) which inserts special tokens into all source sentences to indicate the desired target language. For comparison, we also train bilingual systems that can translate in only one direction each. Our automatic evaluation confirms that one multilingual system leads to higher translation quality than individual bilingual systems (see Appendix B.2).

4.4 Language Dependent Implementation

In this paper, we study three sign languages: LIS-CH, LSF-CH and DSGS. For LIS-CH and LSF-CH we always apply our simple lemmatizer (§4.1) for the text-to-gloss step. The lemmatizer-only component is universally applicable to many more languages. However, it is worth noting that this approach does not capture the full spectrum of syntactic and morphological changes necessary in going from a spoken language to a sign language, which likely leads to suboptimal translations.

For DSGS, we explored different options for text-to-gloss, comparing the lemmatizer (§4.1), rule-based system (§4.2) and NMT system (§4.3). We observed that the glosses output by the NMT system are less accurate than rule-based reordering. A potential explanation for this is that the system is trained on German Sign Language (DGS) data. Due to the inherent differences between DGS and DSGS, using the NMT system could result in inaccurate translations or out-of-lexicon glosses. Furthermore, we found that the NMT system is not robust to out-of-domain text or capitalization differences, which further limits its applicability in these scenarios.

In the end, for DSGS we opted to employ our rule-based system (§4.2), which has been tailored to accommodate the unique linguistic characteristics of DSGS, and produces the best results.

5 Gloss-to-Pose

Gloss-to-pose translation involves converting sign language glosses into a sequence of poses that adequately represent a sequence of signs.

We use the SignSuisse dataset (Schweizerischer Gehörlosenbund SGB-FSS, 2023), which consists of sign language videos in three different languages. We extract skeletal poses from these videos using Mediapipe Holistic (Grishchenko and Bazarevsky, 2020), a state-of-the-art pose estimation framework that estimates 3D coordinates of various landmarks on the human body, including the face, hands, and body. We preprocess the poses by ensuring that the `body` wrists are in the same location as the `hand` wrists, removing the legs, hands, and face from the body pose, and cropping the videos in the beginning and end to avoid returning to a neutral body position.

We concatenate the poses for each gloss by finding the best 'stitching' point that minimizes L2 distance. We then concatenate these poses, adding 0.2 seconds of 'padding' in between, before applying cubic smoothing on each joint to ensure smooth transitions between signs, and filling in missing keypoints. Finally, we apply a Savitzky-Golay motion transition smoothing filter (Savitzky and Golay, 1964), similar to Stoll et al. (2020), to reduce unnatural motion.

6 Pose-to-Video

We use a semi-realistic human-like avatar system to animate the poses generated by our approach. The avatar system is a Pix2Pix model (Isola et al., 2016) adjusted to operate on pose sequences, not individual images. With her permission, we use the likeness of Maayan Gazuli[2]. We use OpenCV (Bradski, 2000) to render the poses as images and feed them into the Pix2Pix model to generate realistic-looking video frames. The avatar system can run in real-time on supported devices and is integrated into `https://sign.mt` (Moryossef, 2023). This system is far from the state of the art, however, we believe that the open-source nature of it will bring rapid improvements, like faster inference speed, and higher animation quality.

7 Future Work

Here we include several future work directions that we believe have the potential to further enhance the performance and user experience of our system for text-to-gloss-to-pose-to-video generation, and we look forward to exploring these possibilities in the future, together with the open-source community.

[2] `https://nlp.biu.ac.il/~amit/datasets/GreenScreen/`

Before	$INDEX1 ENDE1^ ANDERS1* SEHEN1 MÜNCHEN1B* BEREICH1A*
After	$INDEX1 ENDE1 ANDERS1 SEHEN1 MÜNCHEN1 BEREICH1
Before	ICH1 ETWAS-PLANEN-UND-UMSETZEN1 SELBST1A* KLAPPT1* $GEST-OFF^ BIS-JETZT1 GEWOHNHEIT1* $GEST-OFF^*
After	ICH1 ETWAS-PLANEN-UND-UMSETZEN1 SELBST1 KLAPPT1 BIS-JETZT1 GEWOHNHEIT1

Table 2: Examples for preprocessing of DGS glosses.

7.1 Qualitative Evaluation

To evaluate the effectiveness of our approach, we will conduct a study to gather first impressions from deaf users. We already recruited a group of deaf individuals and will ask them to use our system to translate text into sign language videos.

Each participant will be asked to provide feedback on the system after using it to translate five different sentences from German into DSGS. We will provide the sentences to the participants, and they will be asked to sign the translations generated by our system. After each sentence, the participant will be asked to provide feedback on the accuracy of the translation, the quality of the poses and/or synthesized video, and the overall usability of the system.

7.2 Gloss Sense Disambiguation

The current approach to text-to-gloss translation relies on a simple lemmatizer and a rule-based word reordering and dropping component, which can lead to ambiguity in the glosses produced. In the future, we can enhance our system by incorporating gloss sense disambiguation to better capture the intended meaning of the input text. Our NMT approach responds with gloss IDs from the MeineDGS corpus, which already are sense-disambiguated. Annotation of our sign language lexicon with senses will allow us to retrieve the relevant sense.

7.3 Handling Unknown Glosses

Where we encounter a gloss that does not exist in our lexicon, we propose exploring alternative methods to generate a video for it. One possible solution is to leverage another lexicon that includes a written representation of the gloss in question (e.g., SignWriting (Sutton, 1990) or HamNoSys (Prillwitz and Zienert, 1990)), or to employ a neural machine translation system to translate the individual concept to a writing system. Utilizing the capabilities of machine translation to embed words, we can perform a fuzzy match, addressing issues such as synonyms.

Additionally, for named entities such as proper nouns and place names that are not covered by our current gloss-to-pose conversion system, we could revert to fingerspelling them.

Once we have the written representation, we can use a system like Ham2Pose (Shalev-Arkushin et al., 2023) to generate a single sign video from the writing. When combined with fingerspelling for named entities, this approach should enable greater coverage of the language.

7.4 Handling Unknown Gloss Variations

In situations where the required gloss variation is not present in the lexicon but a related gloss exists, we propose developing a system that can modify the known gloss to generate the desired variation. This would allow for better handling of unknown gloss variations and increase the accuracy of the information conveyed by the signing.

7.4.1 Number Forms

For words like *KINDER* (children), we may encounter glosses such as *KIND+*, which represent "child" in plural form. Assuming that we have *KIND* in our lexicon but not *KINDER*, a system could be developed to modify signs to plural forms, such as by repeating movements or incorporating specific handshapes or locations that indicate plurality in the target sign language. Conversely, if we only have the plural form of a gloss in our lexicon, the system could be designed to generate the singular form by removing or modifying the elements that indicate plurality.

7.4.2 Part of Speech Conversion

Another challenge arises when nouns or verbs exist in the lexicon, but their counterparts do not. For instance, if *HELFEN* (to help) is present in the dictionary as a verb, but *HILFE* (help) does not exist as a noun, a system could be designed to modify signs from one part of speech to another, such as from verb to noun or noun to verb.

This system could potentially involve morphological or movement modifications, depending on the linguistic rules of the target sign language.

7.5 Post-editing Pose Sequences

The current approach generates a sequence of poses that represent a sign language sentence. We believe that there is also room for improvement in terms of the fluency and naturalness of the generated sequence. Exploring the use of automatic post-editing techniques is necessary. One such approach could identify datasets that include sentences and gloss sequences, such as the Public DGS Corpus, then, using our gloss-to-pose approach generate a pose sequence with poses from the lexicon, and could learn a diffusion model between the synthetic and real pose sequences.

8 Conclusions

We presented an implementation of a text-to-gloss-to-pose-to-video pipeline for sign language translation, focusing on Swiss German Sign Language, Swiss French Sign Language, and Swiss Italian Sign Language. Our approach comprises three main components: text-to-gloss translation, gloss-to-pose conversion, and pose-to-video animation.

We explained the structure of our system and discussed its limitations, as well as future work directions to address them. These directions have the potential to improve our system, and we look forward to exploring them in collaboration with the open-source community.

The main contribution of this paper is the creation of a reproducible baseline for spoken to signed language translation. The system should serve as a baseline for comparison with more sophisticated sign language translation systems and can be improved upon by the community. You can try our system for the three signed languages of Switzerland on `https://sign.mt`.

Acknowledgements

This work was funded by the EU Horizon 2020 project EASIER (grant agreement no. 101016982), the Swiss Innovation Agency (Innosuisse) flagship IICT (PFFS-21-47), and the EU Horizon 2020 project iEXTRACT (grant agreement no. 802774).

References

Abeillé, Anne, Yves Schabes, and Aravind K Joshi. 1991. Using lexicalized tags for machine translation. Technical Report MS-CIS-91-44, University of Pennsylvania Department of Computer and Information Sciences.

Barbaresi, Adrien. 2023. Simplemma, January.

Bradski, G. 2000. The OpenCV Library. *Dr. Dobb's Journal of Software Tools*.

Camgöz, Necati Cihan, Simon Hadfield, Oscar Koller, Hermann Ney, and Richard Bowden. 2018. Neural sign language translation. In *Proceedings of the IEEE Conference on Computer Vision and Pattern Recognition*, pages 7784–7793.

Cao, Z., G. Hidalgo Martinez, T. Simon, S. Wei, and Y. A. Sheikh. 2019. OpenPose: Realtime Multi-Person 2D Pose Estimation using Part Affinity Fields. *IEEE Transactions on Pattern Analysis and Machine Intelligence*.

Chan, Caroline, Shiry Ginosar, Tinghui Zhou, and Alexei A Efros. 2019. Everybody dance now. In *Proceedings of the IEEE International Conference on Computer Vision*, pages 5933–5942.

Egea Gómez, Santiago, Euan McGill, and Horacio Saggion. 2021. Syntax-aware transformers for neural machine translation: The case of text to sign gloss translation. In *Proceedings of the 14th Workshop on Building and Using Comparable Corpora (BUCC 2021)*, pages 18–27, Online (Virtual Mode), September. INCOMA Ltd.

Grishchenko, Ivan and Valentin Bazarevsky. 2020. Mediapipe holistic.

Güler, Rıza Alp, Natalia Neverova, and Iasonas Kokkinos. 2018. Densepose: Dense human pose estimation in the wild. In *Proceedings of the IEEE Conference on Computer Vision and Pattern Recognition*, pages 7297–7306.

Hanke, Thomas, Marc Schulder, Reiner Konrad, and Elena Jahn. 2020. Extending the Public DGS Corpus in size and depth. In *Proceedings of the LREC2020 9th Workshop on the Representation and Processing of Sign Languages: Sign Language Resources in the Service of the Language Community, Technological Challenges and Application Perspectives*, pages 75–82, Marseille, France, May. European Language Resources Association (ELRA).

Hieber, Felix, Michael Denkowski, Tobias Domhan, Barbara Darques Barros, Celina Dong Ye, Xing Niu, Cuong Hoang, Ke Tran, Benjamin Hsu, Maria Nadejde, Surafel Lakew, Prashant Mathur, Anna Currey, and Marcello Federico. 2022. Sockeye 3: Fast neural machine translation with pytorch.

Isola, Phillip, Jun-Yan Zhu, Tinghui Zhou, and Alexei A. Efros. 2016. Image-to-image translation with conditional adversarial networks. *2017 IEEE Conference on Computer Vision and Pattern Recognition (CVPR)*, pages 5967–5976.

Isola, Phillip, Jun-Yan Zhu, Tinghui Zhou, and Alexei A Efros. 2017. Image-to-image translation with conditional adversarial networks. In *Proceedings of the IEEE conference on computer vision and pattern recognition*, pages 1125–1134.

Johnson, Melvin, Mike Schuster, Quoc V. Le, Maxim Krikun, Yonghui Wu, Zhifeng Chen, Nikhil Thorat, Fernanda Viégas, Martin Wattenberg, Greg Corrado, Macduff Hughes, and Jeffrey Dean. 2017. Google's multilingual neural machine translation system: Enabling zero-shot translation. *Transactions of the Association for Computational Linguistics*, 5:339–351.

Konrad, Reiner, Thomas Hanke, Gabriele Langer, Susanne König, Lutz König, Rie Nishio, and Anja Regen. 2022. Public DGS Corpus: Annotation Conventions / Öffentliches DGS-Korpus: Annotationskonventionen, June.

Kudo, Taku. 2018. Subword regularization: Improving neural network translation models with multiple subword candidates. In *Proceedings of the 56th Annual Meeting of the Association for Computational Linguistics (Volume 1: Long Papers)*, pages 66–75, Melbourne, Australia, July. Association for Computational Linguistics.

Kusters, Annelies Maria Jozef, Dai O'Brien, and Maartje De Meulder, 2017. *Innovations in Deaf Studies: Critically Mapping the Field*, pages 1–53. Oxford University Press, United Kingdom.

Lebert, Marie. 2008. Project gutenberg (1971-2008).

Min, Jianyuan and Jinxiang Chai. 2012. Motion graphs++ a compact generative model for semantic motion analysis and synthesis. *ACM Transactions on Graphics (TOG)*, 31(6):1–12.

Montani, Ines, Matthew Honnibal, Matthew Honnibal, Sofie Van Landeghem, Adriane Boyd, Henning Peters, Paul O'Leary McCann, jim geovedi, Jim O'Regan, Maxim Samsonov, György Orosz, Daniël de Kok, Duygu Altinok, Søren Lind Kristiansen, Madeesh Kannan, Raphaël Bournhonesque, Lj Miranda, Peter Baumgartner, Edward, Explosion Bot, Richard Hudson, Raphael Mitsch, Roman, Leander Fiedler, Ryn Daniels, Wannaphong Phatthiyaphaibun, Grégory Howard, Yohei Tamura, and Sam Bozek. 2023. explosion/spaCy: v3.5.0: New CLI commands, language updates, bug fixes and much more, January.

Moryossef, Amit and Mathias Müller. 2021. pose-format: Library for viewing, augmenting, and handling .pose files. `https://github.com/sign-language-processing/pose`.

Moryossef, Amit, Kayo Yin, Graham Neubig, and Yoav Goldberg. 2021. Data augmentation for sign language gloss translation. In *Proceedings of the 1st International Workshop on Automatic Translation for Signed and Spoken Languages (AT4SSL)*, pages 1–11, Virtual, August. Association for Machine Translation in the Americas.

Moryossef, Amit. 2023. sign.mt: A web-based application for real-time multilingual sign language translation. `https://sign.mt/`.

Müller, Mathias, Zifan Jiang, Amit Moryossef, Annette Rios, and Sarah Ebling. 2022. Considerations for meaningful sign language machine translation based on glosses. *arXiv preprint arXiv:2211.15464*.

Napier, Jemina and Lorraine Leeson. 2016. *Sign Language in Action*. Palgrave Macmillan, London.

Othman, Achraf and Mohamed Jemni. 2012. English-asl gloss parallel corpus 2012: Aslg-pc12. In *5th Workshop on the Representation and Processing of Sign Languages: Interactions between Corpus and Lexicon LREC*.

Papineni, Kishore, Salim Roukos, Todd Ward, and Wei-Jing Zhu. 2002. Bleu: a method for automatic evaluation of machine translation. In *Proceedings of the 40th Annual Meeting of the Association for Computational Linguistics*, pages 311–318, Philadelphia, Pennsylvania, USA, July. Association for Computational Linguistics.

Pizzuto, Elena Antinoro, Paolo Rossini, and Tommaso Russo. 2006. Representing signed languages in written form: Questions that need to be posed. In Vettori, Chiara, editor, *Proceedings of the LREC2006 2nd Workshop on the Representation and Processing of Sign Languages: Lexicographic Matters and Didactic Scenarios*, pages 1–6, Genoa, Italy, May. European Language Resources Association (ELRA).

Popović, Maja. 2016. chrF deconstructed: beta parameters and n-gram weights. In *Proceedings of the First Conference on Machine Translation: Volume 2, Shared Task Papers*, pages 499–504, Berlin, Germany, August. Association for Computational Linguistics.

Post, Matt. 2018. A call for clarity in reporting BLEU scores. In *Proceedings of the Third Conference on Machine Translation: Research Papers*, pages 186–191, Brussels, Belgium, October. Association for Computational Linguistics.

Press, Ofir and Lior Wolf. 2017. Using the output embedding to improve language models. In *Proceedings of the 15th Conference of the European Chapter of the Association for Computational Linguistics: Volume 2, Short Papers*, pages 157–163, Valencia, Spain, April. Association for Computational Linguistics.

Prillwitz, Siegmund and Heiko Zienert. 1990. Hamburg notation system for sign language: Development of a sign writing with computer application. In *Current trends in European Sign Language Research. Proceedings of the 3rd European Congress on Sign Language Research*, pages 355–379.

Saunders, Ben, Necati Cihan Camgöz, and Richard Bowden. 2020. Everybody sign now: Translating spoken language to photo realistic sign language video. *arXiv preprint arXiv:2011.09846*.

Saunders, Ben, Necati Cihan Camgöz, and Richard Bowden. 2021. Anonysign: Novel human appearance synthesis for sign language video anonymisation. In *2021 16th IEEE International Conference on Automatic Face and Gesture Recognition (FG 2021)*, pages 1–8.

Savitzky, Abraham and Marcel JE Golay. 1964. Smoothing and differentiation of data by simplified least squares procedures. *Analytical chemistry*, 36(8):1627–1639.

Schweizerischer Gehörlosenbund SGB-FSS. 2023. Gehörlosenbund Gebärdensprache-Lexikon. `https://signsuisse.sgb-fss.ch/`. Accessed on: May 28, 2023.

Sennrich, Rico and Biao Zhang. 2019. Revisiting low-resource neural machine translation: A case study. In *Proceedings of the 57th Annual Meeting of the Association for Computational Linguistics*, pages 211–221, Florence, Italy, July. Association for Computational Linguistics.

Shalev-Arkushin, Rotem, Amit Moryossef, and Ohad Fried. 2023. Ham2pose: Animating sign language notation into pose sequences.

Shieber, Stuart and Yves Schabes. 1990. Synchronous tree-adjoining grammars. In *Proceedings of the 13th international conference on computational linguistics*. Association for Computational Linguistics.

Shieber, Stuart M. 1994. Restricting the weak-generative capacity of synchronous tree-adjoining grammars. *Computational Intelligence*, 10(4):371–385.

Stoll, Stephanie, Necati Cihan Camgöz, Simon Hadfield, and Richard Bowden. 2018. Sign language production using neural machine translation and generative adversarial networks. In *Proceedings of the 29th British Machine Vision Conference (BMVC 2018)*. British Machine Vision Association.

Stoll, Stephanie, Necati Cihan Camgöz, Simon Hadfield, and Richard Bowden. 2020. Text2sign: towards sign language production using neural machine translation and generative adversarial networks. *International Journal of Computer Vision*, pages 1–18.

Sutton, Valerie. 1990. *Lessons in sign writing*. SignWriting.

Tiedemann, Jörg and Santhosh Thottingal. 2020. OPUS-MT — Building open translation services for the World. In *Proceedings of the 22nd Annual Conferenec of the European Association for Machine Translation (EAMT)*, Lisbon, Portugal.

Vaswani, Ashish, Noam Shazeer, Niki Parmar, Jakob Uszkoreit, Llion Jones, Aidan N Gomez, Łukasz Kaiser, and Illia Polosukhin. 2017. Attention is All you Need. In *Advances in Neural Information Processing Systems 30*, pages 5998–6008.

Ventura, Lucas, Amanda Cardoso Duarte, and Xavier Giró-i-Nieto. 2020. Can everybody sign now? exploring sign language video generation from 2d poses. *CoRR*, abs/2012.10941.

Wang, Ting-Chun, Ming-Yu Liu, Jun-Yan Zhu, Guilin Liu, Andrew Tao, Jan Kautz, and Bryan Catanzaro. 2018. Video-to-video synthesis. In *Advances in Neural Information Processing Systems (NeurIPS)*.

Yin, Kayo and Jesse Read. 2020. Better sign language translation with STMC-transformer. In *Proceedings of the 28th International Conference on Computational Linguistics*, pages 5975–5989, Barcelona, Spain (Online), December. International Committee on Computational Linguistics.

Zhao, Liwei, Karin Kipper, William Schuler, Christian Vogler, Norman Badler, and Martha Palmer. 2000. A machine translation system from English to American Sign Language. In *Conference of the Association for Machine Translation in the Americas*, pages 54–67. Springer.

A SacreBLEU Signatures

BLEU with internal tokenization	`BLEU+case.mixed+numrefs.1+smooth.exp+tok.13a+version.1.4.14`
BLEU without internal tokenization	`BLEU+case.mixed+numrefs.1+smooth.exp+tok.none+version.1.4.14`
CHRF	`chrF2+numchars.6+space.false+version.1.4.14`

Table 3: SacreBLEU signatures for evaluation metrics.

B Corpus-specific Loading and Gloss Preprocessing

In general, we provide tools to automatically download all relevant examples from the corpus websites and only keep examples that have both a spoken language translation and a gloss transcription. We experiment with corpus-specific preprocessing for glosses, informed by sign language linguistics and the glossing conventions of the corpora.

B.1 DGS Corpus

We download and process release 3.0 of the corpus. To DGS glosses we apply the following modifications derived from the DGS Corpus transcription conventions (Konrad et al., 2022):

- Removing entirely two specific gloss types that cannot possibly help the translation: `$GEST-OFF` and `$$EXTRA-LING-MAN`.
- Removing *ad-hoc* deviations from citation forms, marked by $\star$. Example: `ANDERS1*` → `ANDERS1`.
- Removing the distinction between type glosses and subtype glosses, marked by ^. Example: `WISSEN2B^` → `WISSEN2B`.
- Collapsing phonological variations of the same type that are meaning-equivalent. Such variants are marked with uppercase letter suffixes. Example: `WISSEN2B` → `WISSEN2`.
- Deliberately keep numerals (`$NUM`), list glosses (`$LIST`) and finger alphabet (`$ALPHA`) intact, except for removing handshape variants.

See Table 2 for examples for this preprocessing step. Overall these simplifications should reduce the number of observed forms while not affecting the machine translation task. For other purposes such as linguistic analysis our preprocessing would of course be detrimental.

B.2 Evaluation: Text-to-Gloss NMT

We perform an automatic evaluation of translation quality. We measure translation quality with BLEU (Papineni et al., 2002) and CHRF (Popović, 2016), computed with the tool SacreBLEU (Post, 2018). See Table 3 in Appendix A for all SacreBLEU signatures.

Whenever gloss output is evaluated we disable BLEU's internal tokenization, as advocated by Müller et al. (2022). Earlier works did not consider this detail and therefore our BLEU scores may appear low in comparison.

Finally, because DGS glosses are preprocessed in a corpus-specific way (see above), they are evaluated against a preprocessed reference as well, since this process cannot be reversed after translation. This means that corpus-specific preprocessing for DGS glosses simplifies the translation task overall, compared to a system that predicts glosses in their original forms.

Table 4 reports the translation quality of our machine translation systems, as measured by CHRF. The table shows that one multilingual system that can translate between DGS and German leads to higher translation quality than two bilingual systems.

	DGS→DE	DE→DGS
Bilingual	28.610	-
Bilingual	-	32.920
Multilingual: all DE and DGS directions	28.210	34.760

Table 4: CHRF scores of the multilingual translation system compared to bilingual systems.

Short Papers

A New English-Dutch-NGT Corpus for the Hospitality Domain

Mirella De Sisto
Tilburg University
Netherlands
M.DeSisto@tilburguniversity.edu

Vincent Vandeghinste
Instituut voor de Nederlandse Taal, Leiden
Netherlands
KU Leuven, Belgium
Vincent.Vandeghinste@ivdnt.org

Dimitar Shterionov
Tilburg University
Netherlands
D.Shterionov@tilburguniversity.edu

Abstract

One of the major challenges hampering the development of language technology which targets sign languages is the extremely limited availability of good quality data geared towards machine learning and deep learning approaches. In this paper we introduce the NGT-Dutch Hotel Review Corpus (NGT-HoReCo), which addresses this issue by providing multimodal parallel data in English, Dutch and Sign Language of the Netherlands (NGT). The corpus contains 297 hotel reviews in written English (21.464 words), translated into written Dutch (22.274 words) and into NGT videos (230,54 minutes). It is publicly available through the ELG and the CLARIN platforms.

1 Introduction

As stated in Rivera Pastor et al. (2017), "The emergence of new technological approaches such as deep-learning neural networks, based on increased computational power and access to sizeable amounts of data, are making Human Language Technologies (HLT) a real solution to overcoming language barriers." Nevertheless, these very promising advances mainly concern HLT which focuses on spoken languages only, while HLT which targets sign languages is severely limited and strongly lagging behind (Vandeghinste et al., 2023).

This discrepancy between what has been achieved for spoken languages and what is available for signed languages is due to a number of challenges which are limiting the development of LT for signed languages (e.g. the lack of standardised data format, the lack of a standardised writing and annotation systems, etc.). For more details, see De Sisto et al. (2022).

The biggest bottleneck limiting the performance of new technological approaches for sign languages is the *quantity* of high quality data. To give an example, on average the data available for a relatively well resourced sign language is roughly ten times smaller than data available for a so-called low resource spoken language (Vandeghinste et al., forthcoming).

Besides the quantitative bottleneck, there is also an issue with data *quality*. Besides data scarcity, most of the parallel datasets which are available consist of spoken language news broadcasts interpreted into a sign language (in most cases by a hearing interpreter) (Camgoz et al., 2018). This affects the authenticity and the quality of the sign language data, since the interpreting process interferes with its accuracy (interpretation takes place simultaneously, which means that the interpreter needs to be quick and sometimes has to sacrifice accuracy for efficiency), and most hearing interpreters are not L1 users of the sign language (an exception being interpreters who are CODA — Children of Deaf Adults —and other specific cases).

The goal of the compilation of the NGT-Dutch Hotel Review Corpus (NGT-HoReCo) described in this paper is to contribute to reducing the scarcity of good quality sign language data by providing a multimodal parallel corpus of written English reviews and their translations into written Dutch and into NGT videos. The quality is ensured with respect to the authenticity of the NGT by the fact that translations were performed by deaf professional translators. The accuracy of the translations is ensured by the fact that it concerns actual translations, performed in an offline modus without the constraints which are custom in an interpreting context.

The availability of a corpus such as NGT-HoReCo targets the stimulation of advancements in the field of sign language technology through both high-quality data for training models as well as a gold standard data for evaluation.

2 Related work

EASIER's Deliverable 6.1 (Kopf et al., 2021) and Morgan et al. (2022) provide an overview of the resources available for European sign languages.

NGT, together with German Sign Language (DGS), represent the richest sign languages in Europe in terms of available resources. Nevertheless, data available even for relatively well-represented sign languages are far from being sufficient for the development of language technologies.

The main source of data for NGT is the Corpus NGT (Crasborn et al., 2020), which is available for download at the Language Archive (`https://archive.mpi.nl/tla/`), in the form of separate files, and as a single file through the CLARIN infrastructure (`http://hdl.handle.net/10032/tm-a2-u5`). It contains 72 hours of dialogues between native users of NGT. 104 signers took part to the recordings. One limitation of the corpus is that only 25% of the data have been annotated (Crasborn et al., 2020); this is due to the fact that to date annotation is a manual and very-time consuming task (Morgan et al., 2022). As a consequence, only part of the Corpus NGT can be employed for MT tasks.

A different type of resource is constituted by lexicons. The lexicon of the Corpus NGT (Crasborn et al, 2020a) was made available by Global Signbank and is downloadable per sign. It consists of 3.645 short video files. Another available NGT lexicon downloadable per sign is `https://www.lerengebaren.nl/`, which consists of 2.993 videos.

3 Methodology: Preparation of the corpus

The creation of NGT-HoReCo required preparation of data for both Dutch and NGT. After gathering the publicly available English texts, these were translated into written Dutch; subsequently, the Dutch texts were translated offline into NGT videos by professional deaf translators.

3.1 Translation from English into Dutch

Written English is the source language of the hotel reviews from a Booking.com review corpus publicly available on Kaggle.[1] Reviews were selected with an initial manual screening which ensured that the texts were grammatically complete and correct, and that the text did not contain uncommon abbreviations. In some reviews with incomplete endings, final incomplete sentences were removed and the review was kept, when removal did not affect the meaning of the whole text; alternatively, the whole review ending in an incomplete sentence was removed.

The Dutch text side of the parallel corpus was produced by a professional translation company which used automatic translation (generated by DeepL) following and in-depth human post-editing.

The DeepL translations of the 297 reviews consists of 21.614 words, the post-edited version consists of 22.284 words.[2] An example entry is shown in Table 1.

3.2 Translation from Dutch into Sign Language of the Netherlands

The Dutch-NGT translation was performed by six professional deaf translators. The choice of having only deaf translators performing the task was made in order to ensure that the signing would be authentic and to reduce as much as possible the influence of the source language. For more details about why to use deaf translators, see Vandeghinste et al. (forthcoming). Translators were asked to sign an informed consent form which allows the data to be available under a CC BY-NC license.[3]

Each translation was recorded in a separate video file. Each review was translated once by a single translator.

An excel spreadsheet contains the written side of the parallel corpus: a column containing the English source, a column containing the DeepL translation, a column containing the post-edited version

[1] `https://www.kaggle.com/datasets/datafiniti/hotel-reviews`

[2] Calculated using the linux `wc` command.

[3] The project received ethical clearance from the Research Ethics and Data Management Committee of Tilburg University

Source	All in all the stay was good , but they were having issues with the elevator which was not good for being put on the 3rd floor
DeepL	Al met al was het verblijf goed, maar ze hadden problemen met de lift die niet goed was voor de 3e verdieping.
Video file	`NGT-HoReCo_1`
Post-edit	Al met al was het verblijf goed, maar ze hadden problemen met de lift, wat niet fijn is als je op de 3e verdieping wordt geplaatst.

Table 1: Example entry with its translation by DeepL and the post-edited version

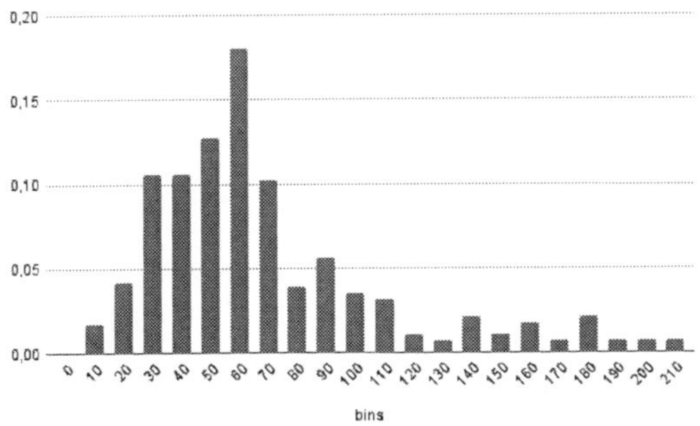

Figure 1: Length distribution of the post-edited Dutch translations, in bins of 10 words

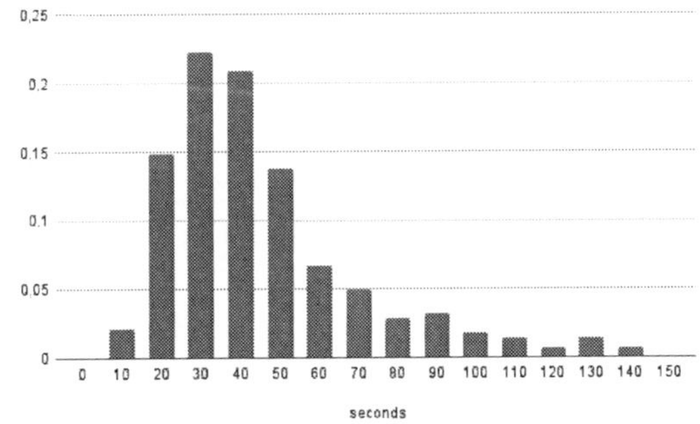

Figure 2: Length distribution of the video files in bins of 10 seconds

and a column containing the name of the corresponding NGT video file.

4 Results: NGT-HoReCo

The corpus comprises 297 hotel reviews (roughly 1.680 sentences) in written English, their translation into written Dutch and into NGT videos. The limited domain of the data, namely, hospitality, allows to have recurrent topics and signs in different possible combinations and to account, to a certain extent, for inter and intra signer variation.

The total amounts of words contained in the corpus is 21.464 for English and 22.274 for the Dutch text. The word length of the written reviews varies from around 15 to 400 words. The distribution of lengths in the post-edited translation is presented in Figure 1, where the X-axis is the length of the post-edited text, in bins of 10 words. The Y-axis is the ratio of files with a certain length.

The NGT translations consist of almost 4 hours of videos (230,54 minutes). The duration of the NGT videos ranges from around 10 seconds to around 4 minutes. The distribution of lengths of the videos is presented in Figure 2, where the Y-axis is the ratio of files and the X-axis is the duration in seconds, in bins of 10 seconds.

The corpus is publicly available through the ELG platform at `https://live.european-language-grid.eu/catalogue/corpus/21566`, and is also made available through the CLARIN platform. The permanent identifier for corpus download is `http://hdl.handle.net/10032/tm-a2-w2`. NGT-HoReCo is available under a CC BY-NC license, however, the written English text does not have availability restrictions, being fully publicly available in a Kaggle dataset.

5 Conclusion and future steps

In this paper we introduced a new available multimodal parallel corpus of written English, written Dutch and NGT videos. The corpus contains 297 hotel reviews in written English which were translated into written Dutch and into NGT videos. The Dutch-NGT translations were performed by deaf professional translators.

Parallel data such as NGT-HoReCo support further developments of Sign Language Technology, including but not limited to Sign Language Machine Translation.

A current limitation of the corpus is that there is no alignment between written sentences and video fragments. To date, there are no tools to automatically generate such alignment; consequently, a further implementation of the corpus would include manual alignment.

In addition, the size of the corpus is still quite limited, due to time and cost restrictions of the NGT-HoReCo project.

Nevertheless, the advantage of the availability of parallel data such as NGT-HoReCo is that similar parallel corpora have the potential to be implemented with additional features and languages.

For instance, having the same reviews translated by more NGT translators coming from different parts of the Netherlands would account for language variation. We have considered this option but decided to first focus on having as many reviews translated as possible. Nevertheless, this would be a valuable direction for an implementation of the corpus.

Currently we have initiated a further development of NGT-HoReCo to also include Flemish Sign Language (VGT). Adding VGT is of particular interest because NGT and VGT, despite not being closely related languages, both base their mouthing on Dutch and are generally used in countries where Dutch is (one of) the official language(s). Additionally, NGT-HoReCo is going to be enriched with different types of annotations, such as pose estimates, etc.

Acknowledgments

The NGT-HoReCo project was funded by the European Language Equality 2 project (ELE 2), which has received funding from the European Union under the grant agreement no. LC-01884166 – 101075356 (ELE 2).

Work in this paper is part of the SignON project.[4] This project has received funding from the European Union's Horizon 2020 Research and Innovation Programme under Grant Agreement No. 101017255.

References

Camgoz, Necati Cihan, Simon Hadfield, Oscar Koller, Hermann Ney, and Richard Bowden. 2018. Neural sign language translation. In *Proceedings of the IEEE conference on Computer Vision and Pattern Recognition (CVPR)*, Salt Lake City, USA, 18 – 22 June. IEEE.

Crasborn, O., I. Zwitserlood, J. Ros, and M. van Zuilen. 2020. Corpus ngt, 4e editie.

De Sisto, Mirella, Vincent Vandeghinste, Santiago Egea Gómez, Mathieu De Coster, Dimitar Shterionov, and Horacio Saggion. 2022. Challenges with sign language datasets for sign language recognition and translation. In *Proceedings of the Thirteenth Language Resources and Evaluation Conference*, pages 2478–2487, Marseille, France, June. European Language Resources Association.

Kopf, Maria, Marc Schulder, and Thomas Hanke. 2021. Overview of datasets for the sign languages of europe. Deliverable 6.1, Easier project.

Morgan, Hope E., Onno Crasborn, Maria Kopf, Marc Schulder, and Thomas Hanke. 2022. Facilitating the spread of new sign language technologies across Europe. In Efthimiou, Eleni, Stavroula-Evita Fotinea, Thomas Hanke, Julie A. Hochgesang, Jette Kristoffersen, Johanna Mesch, and Marc Schulder, editors, *Proceedings of the LREC2022 10th workshop on the representation and processing of sign languages: Multilingual sign language resources*, pages 144–147, Marseille, France. European Language Resources Association (ELRA).

Rivera Pastor, Rafael, Carlota Tarín Quirós, Juan Pablo Villar García, Toni Badia Cardús, and Maite Melero Nogués. 2017. Language equality in the digital age – Towards a Human Language Project. STOA study (PE 598.621), IP/G/STOA/FWC/2013-001/Lot4/C2, March 2017. Carried out by Iclaves SL (Spain) at the request of the Science and Technology Options Assessment (STOA) Panel, managed by the Scientific Foresight Unit (STOA), within the Directorate-General for Parliamentary Research Services (DG EPRS) of the European Parliament, March. `https://www.europarl.europa.eu/thinktank/en/document/EPRS_STU(2017)598621`.

Vandeghinste, Vincent, Mirella De Sisto, Maria Kopf, Marc Schulder, Caro Brosens, Lien Soetemans, Rehana Omardeen, Frankie Picron, Davy Van Landuyt, Irene Murtagh, Elefterios Avramidis, and Mathieu De Coster. 2023. Report on Europe's Sign Languages. Technical report, European Language Equality D1.40.

Vandeghinste, Vincent, Mirella De Sisto, Santiago Egea Gomez, and Mathieu De Coster. forthcoming. Challenges with sign language datasets. In Way, Andy, Dimitar Shterionov, Lorraine Leeson, and Christian Rathmann, editors, *Sign Language Machine Translation*, chapter 10, pages 266–290. Springer, Oxford.

[4] `https://signon-project.eu`

BSL-Hansard: A parallel, multimodal corpus of English and interpreted British Sign Language data from parliamentary proceedings

Euan McGill
Universitat Pompeu Fabra
Barcelona, Spain
euan.mcgill@upf.edu

Horacio Saggion
Universitat Pompeu Fabra
Barcelona, Spain
horacio.saggion@upf.edu

Abstract

BSL-Hansard is a novel open source and multimodal resource composed by combining Sign Language video data in BSL and English text from the official transcription of British parliamentary sessions. This paper describes the method followed to compile BSL-Hansard including time alignment of text using the MAUS (Schiel, 2015) segmentation system, gives some statistics about this dataset, and suggests experiments. These primarily include end-to-end Sign Language-to-text translation, but is also relevant for broader machine translation, and speech and language processing tasks.

1 Introduction

In the United Kingdom (UK), there are an estimated 151,000 British Sign Language (BSL) signers according to the British Deaf Association[1] many of whom constitute the d/Deaf and Hard-of-Hearing (DHH) community in that country. BSL is a flourishing language, and has seen a 40% increase in the number of people who identify their main language as BSL in the ten years between the 2011 and 2021 Census in England and Wales[2].

d/Deaf signers prefer to access information and use technology in their native language (Yin et al., 2021) which is, in many cases, a sign language (SL). However, technologies such as machine translation (MT) for sign languages (SLT) are much less well-established compared to their spoken language counterparts (Bragg et al., 2019; Núñez-Marcos et al., 2023). This means that many DHH individuals must opt for resources in their non-primary language, often the ambient spoken language in the territory - for example English where BSL is used.

In recent years, there has been marked progress in the provision of information and services for BSL signers. For example, a growing proportion of public service television broadcasting is available with BSL interpretation and members of the DHH community are becoming more prominent in the national media[3]. The recent British Sign Language Act 2022 has also enshrined in law BSL's status as an official language of England, Scotland, and Wales. However, there remains a comparatively small amount of data available to develop language technology resources for BSL. The BSL-Hansard dataset intends to make a large amount of parallel English-BSL data available to researchers.

Section 2 explores resources available for BSL, before Sections 3 and 4 introduce and describe the parallel BSL-Hansard dataset of English-BSL parliamentary utterances. Section 5 then discusses possible uses and experiments with the dataset, and offers concluding remarks.

2 BSL resources

There is already a body of extant resources available for SLT research using BSL. Perhaps the most prominent is the BSL Corpus (Schembri et al., 2013) which is the first digitised corpus of continuous BSL. It contains an impressive amount of vari-

[1]https://bda.org.uk/help-resources/

[2]https://www.ons.gov.uk/peoplepopulationandcommunity/culturalidentity/language/bulletins/languageenglandandwales/census2021#main-languages-varied-across-england-and-wales

[3]https://www.theguardian.com/society/2021/dec/25/rose-ayling-elliss-strictly-come-dancing-win-gives-deaf-children-huge-confidence-boost

ation from elicited and natural conversation, with 249 signers across eight British cities and is intended for a broad range of research tasks. Annotation is currently incomplete, so it is important to pursue other data collection projects. There exist other resources for BSL including the ECHO corpus (Brugman et al., 2004) with sign video and extensive linguistic annotation, and Dicta-Sign[4] which contains isolated sign videos.

Another resource is the BOBSL (Albanie et al., 2021) parallel English-BSL dataset. Similar to BSL-Hansard, BOBSL was created by collating $1,400$h of a broad range of BBC television programmes and their companion BSL interpretation. It is a valuable resource which is large enough to conduct machine learning research, shown by the researchers' experiments on SLT, sign language recognition (SLR), and sentence alignment. However it seems that although the corpus is free to use, each researcher must request access individually which makes it impractical to leverage its data in large, commercial projects (De Sisto et al., 2022).

Other resources may be generated through data augmentation, transfer learning, and bootstrapping techniques from better-resourced SLs such as American Sign Language or from spoken languages (Moryossef et al., 2021; Zhou et al., 2021). This type of data may be suboptimal (Yin and Read, 2020) as they are not a genuine representation of a SL, and the same may be said about data from SL interpretation (Bragg et al., 2021). However, these are currently frequently-utilised ways of obtaining sufficient quantities of data for data-hungry machine learning approaches.

2.1 BSL in Parliament

There has been BSL interpretation for every edition of Prime Minister's Questions (PMQs) and Budget statements in the British House of Commons since early 2020[5]. More recently (since January 2023), the session immediately before PMQs is interpreted. In addition, there are plans to interpret a greater number and wider range of parliamentary from summer 2023 which will provide an even larger amount of parallel data available.

Every session in the UK Parliament is transcribed in English in a "substantially verbatim"[6] manner, and is kept as public record in Hansard. Every session is also publicly available in video and audio on the Parliamentlive.tv web service. As such, this allows for alignment in parallel between BSL video and English text and audio. The following sections first describe the amount of data that is available and used for the purpose of compiling this parallel resource, followed by the method used to compile it, and then a discussion of its use and place in the wider literature.

Figure 1: Signer framing type in SL videos

3 Dataset statistics

BSL-Hansard contains 86h40m of SL video in *.mp4* format from 19 individual signers. There is no additional demographic information, as there is no extant source of the interpreters self-identifying. Appendix 1 shows the amount of sessions interpreted by each signer by alias, as well as a suggested split into train, development, and test splits whereby no individual signer appears in more than one of these sets. The exact split is 62% for training, 18% for development, and 20% for test. These sets are slightly uneven due to the fact that some signers co-appear in some videos.

The videos frame the signer in two distinct ways, shown in Figure 1. The first separates the signer into a box with a plain background (left), which takes up approximately one third of the video frame. The second superimposes the signer in the bottom right-hand corner of the screen over a mixture of footage from partially the parliamentary chamber and partially a plain background (right). There are 34 instances of the former type in the corpus, and 78 instances of the latter.

The accompanying transcripts total 871k words in English, which are aligned on timestamped sentences to the appropriate video. There are 18.9k unique words where 4.6k overlap with the large SignBSL[7] dictionary resource. The most frequently-occurring non-stopword in the dataset is "prime" which appears 8.7k times. There are 112 individual sessions, and the nine session types

[4]https://www.sign-lang.uni-hamburg.de/dicta-sign/portal/

[5]https://www.parliament.uk/business/news

[6]As well as text on parliamentary procedure, "members' words are recorded, and then edited to remove repetitions and obvious mistakes, albeit without taking away from the meaning of what is said" (https://hansard.parliament.uk/)

[7]https://www.signbsl.com/about

are distinguished by video and transcript titles in the dataset. Appendix 1 provides information about the types of parliamentary session which make up the dataset and define how the files are labelled.

4 Dataset compilation

Videos in *.mp4* format are manually downloaded from the Parliamentlive.tv web service, and the official transcripts are manually downloaded from the Hansard web page.

The videos and texts are then processed predominantly using the functionality of the Munich Automatic Segmentation System (MAUS) (Schiel, 2015). MAUS is a Hidden Markov Model-based statistical forced aligner which first predicts the phonetic label based on an input transcript, and then aligns the predicted phones with an input audio signal. This service is available on the web (Kisler et al., 2017), and can be used with other functionalities such as pre-processing, grapheme-to-phoneme conversion, and subtitle generation.

Figure 2 provides an overview of the processing tasks and file types involved. A given input video with a maximum duration of no more than nine minutes is matched with the appropriate Hansard transcript, and converted to *.wav* format using the *ffmpeg* library. The input text is pre-processed by removing all content inside parentheses and square brackets, as well as the first three lines of procedure in each Hansard document.

The resulting *.txt* and *.wav* files are input into the 'WebMAUS Basic'[8] web service where the British English language model is chosen, and output format is set to *.bpf* - a file type which allows for time alignment between the phonetic transcription and the audio signal.

The text file containing the original transcription and the aligned *.bpf* file are subsequently input into the BAS 'Subtitle'[9] web tool which maps the alignment with the original transcript in order to generate sentence-type utterances. In order to preserve full phrases as well as possible, the parameters are set to split subtitles on punctuation marks, or otherwise at a maximum length of 20 words - the result is output to *.vtt* file format. These files may be converted to a researcher-friendly *.csv* or *.json* formats by means of straightforward, freely-available conversion scripts[10].

4.1 Dataset storage, usage and reproducibility

This dataset is stored as open access in a Zenodo[11] repository. The processing scripts and tools, as well as tools to isolate the signer in both framing types, are stored in a Github repository[12].

BSL-Hansard is stored in this way due to the terms of use[13] of the UK Parliament's web services. It is possible to store excerpts of parliamentary sessions in a manner available to everyone, but in context and without editing or manipulating the video or audio feeds in any way. It also allows this resource to be available on a platform which is robust and secure.

5 Uses, discussion and future steps

It is possible for researchers, particularly those on machine translation between signed and spoken languages, to use BSL-Hansard in many ways. This section describes some experiments that are possible to conduct with this data, and experiments that will improve the data inside the dataset. It also describes some of the limitations of the dataset and this type of dataset in general. Finally, there is a brief note on the extensibility of this dataset and the methods used to compile it before some concluding remarks.

5.1 Sign Language translation

The first is end-to-end (E2E) sign language translation, in other words going from sign language video directly to text. These methods are based on Transformer encoder-decoder architecture (e.g. (Liu et al., 2020)). A system introduced in Camgöz et al. (2020) can jointly learn SLR and translation, and negates the need to go through an intermediate step of SL gloss-to-text transformation. They achieved state-of-the-art performance at the time on the PHOENIX-Weather (Camgöz et al., 2018) German Sign Language corpus. An interesting next step would be to implement an E2E method using BSL-Hansard videos. The BOBSL

[8] https://clarin.phonetik.uni-muenchen.de/BASWebServices/interface/WebMAUSBasic

[9] https://clarin.phonetik.uni-muenchen.de/BASWebServices/interface/Subtitle

[10] e.g. https://github.com/iTrauco/vtt-to-csv-python-script

[11] https://zenodo.org/record/7974945

[12] https://github.com/LaSTUS-TALN-UPF/BSL-Hansard-tools

[13] https://www.parliament.uk/site-information/copyright-parliament/pru-licence-agreements/downloading–sharing-terms–conditions/

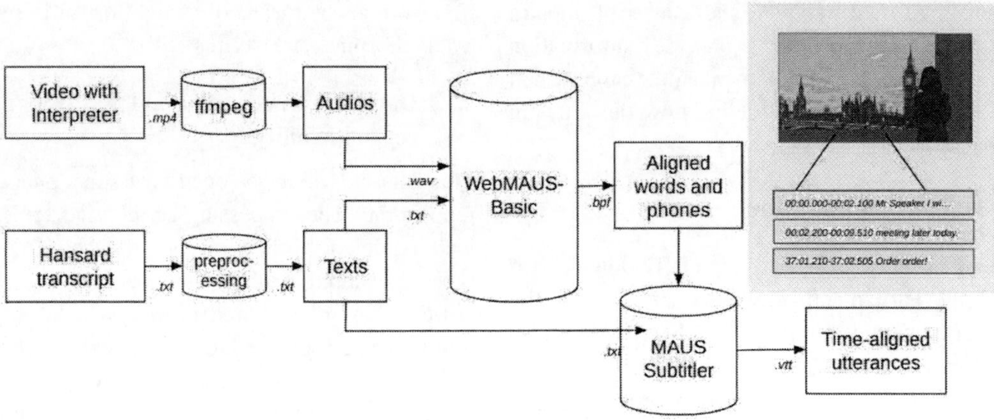

Figure 2: Processing pipeline between input video and text into time-aligned labelled text, including the file input and output types involved. The dataset is made up of the video files and time aligned text captions (pictured, top right).

authors (Albanie et al., 2021) did implement an E2E transformer-based methodology with limited success (1.00 BLEU-4), citing the unconstrained settings, large vocabulary and wide domain of their dataset. It is possible that better results may be achieved on this dataset despite its much smaller size as it is much more domain-specific by only containing parliamentary exchanges.

It may also be beneficial to implement other E2E methods, such as the recent SLTUNET model (Zhang et al., 2023). Also, the STMC transformer (Yin and Read, 2020) has been shown to outperform Camgöz et al. (2020)'s results and to be generalisable to other datasets.

5.2 Annotation, alignment and recognition

As E2E translation is the only translation type possible, due to the SL video not having annotations, it may be beneficial to label this dataset with SL glosses. Fortunately, BSL has rich dictionary resources to draw from with relatively large vocabulary sizes.

Outwith the joint approach in E2E SLT, labelling can be achieved through continuous SLR (Wadhawan and Kumar, 2021). The two different video framing settings may be challenging, but signers are consistently directly facing the camera and dressed in grey formal clothing.

While the dataset is labelled with aligned English text, it is also possible to perform alignment as an automated annotation strategy known as 'sign spotting'. As proposed in Albanie et al. (2020), keywords may be spotted through mouthings (a frequently-used articulator in SL inventories) using computer vision techniques. In addition, signs can be spotted through comparing them to SL lexicons - as previously mentioned, these are well resourced for BSL. Sign spotting may be a fruitful technique for this dataset specifically, as parliamentary procedure makes terms such as 'Mr. Speaker' or 'prime minister' occur very frequently which means these can be used as temporal keypoints for further annotation.

These methods may be considerably less accurate than manual transcription, but are far less human resource-intensive.

5.3 Limitations and opportunities

The main limitation of interpreted SL data, which makes up all of BSL-Hansard, is that it lacks the naturalness and regional (Sutton-Spence and Woll, 1999) and sociolinguistic (Lucas and Bayley, 2016; Schembri et al., 2018) variation of native and conversational BSL. It is also important to note that interpreted SL may not convey the entire message of the spoken language data due to brevity restrictions and errors which naturally occur during live interpretation. That being said, this data is still valuable as the sheer amount of parallel sentences in one domain allow the implementation of machine learning techniques.

This dataset is also readily extensible, as there is a constant and increasing stream of BSL-interpreted parliamentary sessions becoming available. It may also be possible to extend this methodology of dataset compilation into, for example, the Scottish and Catalan Parliaments which both have signed video and official transcripts available to download.

Acknowledgements: This work has been conducted within the SignON project. SignON is a Horizon 2020 project, funded under the Horizon 2020 program ICT-57-2020 - "An empowering, inclusive, Next Generation Internet" with Grant Agreement number 101017255.

We also acknowledge support from the Spanish State Research Agency under the Maria de Maeztu Units of Excellence Programme (CEX2021-001195-M).

References

Albanie, Samuel, Gül Varol, Liliane Momeni, Triantafyllos Afouras, Joon Son Chung, Neil Fox, and Andrew Zisserman. 2020. BSL-1K: Scaling up co-articulated sign language recognition using mouthing cues. In *European Conference on Computer Vision*.

Albanie, Samuel, Gül Varol, Liliane Momeni, Hannah Bull, Triantafyllos Afouras, Himel Chowdhury, Neil Fox, Bencie Woll, Rob Cooper, Andrew McParland, and Andrew Zisserman. 2021. BOBSL: BBC-Oxford British Sign Language Dataset.

Bragg, Danielle, Oscar Koller, Mary Bellard, Larwan Berke, Patrick Boudreault, Annelies Braffort, Naomi Caselli, Matt Huenerfauth, Hernisa Kacorri, Tessa Verhoef, Christian Vogler, and Meredith Ringel Morris. 2019. Sign Language Recognition, Generation, and Translation: An Interdisciplinary Perspective. In *The 21st International ACM SIGACCESS Conference on Computers and Accessibility*, ASSETS '19, page 16–31, New York, NY, USA. Association for Computing Machinery.

Bragg, Danielle, Naomi Caselli, Julie A. Hochgesang, Matt Huenerfauth, Leah Katz-Hernandez, Oscar Koller, Raja Kushalnagar, Christian Vogler, and Richard E. Ladner. 2021. The fate landscape of sign language ai datasets: An interdisciplinary perspective. 14(2):1936–7228.

Brugman, Hennie, Onno Crasborn, and Albert Russel. 2004. Collaborative annotation of sign language data with peer-to-peer technology. In Lino, Maria Teresa, Maria Francisca Xavier, Fátima Ferreira, Rute Costa, and Raquel Silva, editors, *4th International Conference on Language Resources and Evaluation (LREC 2004)*, pages 213–216, Lisbon, Portugal, May. European Language Resources Association (ELRA).

Camgöz, Necati, Simon Hadfield, Oscar Koller, Hermann Ney, and Richard Bowden. 2018. Neural sign language translation. In *CVPR 2018*, pages 7784–7793, 03.

Camgöz, Necati Cihan, Oscar Koller, Simon Hadfield, and Richard Bowden. 2020. Sign language transformers: Joint end-to-end sign language recognition and translation. In *CVPR 2020*, pages 10020–10030.

De Sisto, Mirella, Vincent Vandeghinste, Santiago Egea Gómez, Mathieu De Coster, Dimitar Shterionov, and Horacio Saggion. 2022. Challenges with sign language datasets for sign language recognition and translation. In *Proceedings of the Thirteenth Language Resources and Evaluation Conference*, pages 2478–2487, Marseille, France, June. European Language Resources Association.

Kisler, Thomas, Uwe Reichel, and Florian Schiel. 2017. Multilingual processing of speech via web services. *Computer Speech & Language*, 45:326–347.

Liu et al. 2020. Multilingual denoising pre-training for neural machine translation. *CoRR*, pages 1–17.

Lucas, Ceil and Robert Bayley. 2016. Quantative sociolinguistics and sign languages: Implications for sociolinguistic theory. In Coupland, Nikolas, editor, *Sociolinguistics: Theoretical Debates*, chapter 16, pages 349–366. Cambridge University Press, Cambridge, United Kingdom.

Moryossef, Amit, Kayo Yin, Graham Neubig, and Yoav Goldberg. 2021. Data augmentation for sign language gloss translation.

Núñez-Marcos, Adrián, Olatz Perez de Viñaspre, and Gorka Labaka. 2023. A survey on sign language machine translation. *Expert Systems with Applications*, 213:118993.

Schembri, Adam, Jordan Fenlon, Ramas Rentelis, Sally Reynolds, and Kearsy Cormier. 2013. Building the british sign language corpus. *Language Documentation and Conservation*, 7:136–154.

Schembri, Adam, Rose Stamp, Jordan Fenlon, and Kearsy Cormier. 2018. Variation and change in varieties of british sign language in england. In Braber, Natalie and Sandra Jansen, editors, *Sociolinguistics in England*, chapter 7, pages 165–188. Palgrave Macmillan, London, United Kingdom.

Schiel, Florian. 2015. A statistical model for predicting pronunciation. In *International Congress of Phonetic Sciences*.

Sutton-Spence, R. and B. Woll. 1999. *The Linguistics of British Sign Language: An Introduction*. The Linguistics of British Sign Language: An Introduction. Cambridge University Press.

Wadhawan, Ankita and Parteek Kumar. 2021. Sign language recognition systems: A decade systematic literature review. 28:785–813.

Yin, Kayo and Jesse Read. 2020. Better sign language translation with STMC-transformer. In *COLING 2020*, pages 5975–5989, Online. ICCL.

Yin, Kayo, Amit Moryossef, Julie Hochgesang, Yoav Goldberg, and Malihe Alikhani. 2021. Including signed languages in natural language processing.

Zhang, Biao, Mathias Müller, and Rico Sennrich. 2023. SLTUNET: A simple unified model for sign language translation. In *The Eleventh International Conference on Learning Representations*.

Zhou, Hao, Wengang Zhou, Weizhen Qi, Junfu Pu, and Houqiang Li. 2021. Improving sign language translation with monolingual data by sign back-translation.

Appendix 1: Dataset statistics

Type	Description	Total
PMQs	Prime Minister's Questions	110
Budget	Financial statements/budgets from the Chancellor of the Exchequer	7
Covid	Statements about the Coronavirus pandemic	4
NIQs	Questions to the Secretary of State for Northern Ireland	2
SCQs	Questions to the Secretary of State for Scotland	2
WEQs	Questions to the Minister for Women and Equality	2
AGQs	Questions to the Attorney General	1
CYQs	Questions to the Secretary of State for Wales	1
SITQs	Questions to the Minister for Science Technology and Innovation	1
Afghanistan	Updates on the conflict in Afghanistan	1

Table 1: Session types and frequency in the dataset

Signer	# sessions	Partition
S101	1	Test
S102	16	Train
S103	2	Test
S104	2	Train
S105	1	Dev
S106	1	Test
S107	6	Train
S108	7	Train
S109	3	Train
S201	5	Test
S202	4	Dev
S203	10	Test
S204	15	Dev
S205	24	Train
S207	16	Train
S208	1	Test
S209	1	Train
S210	6	Test
S211	2	Dev

Table 2: Individual signer IDs used in the corpus, number of occurrences in sessions, and place in the dataset partition

Towards Accommodating Gerunds within the Sign Language Lexicon

Zaid Mohammed
School of Informatics and Cybersecurity
Technological University Dublin
Ireland
zaid.mohammed@adaptcentre.ie

Irene Murtagh
School of Informatics and Cybersecurity
Technological University Dublin
Ireland
irene.murtagh@adaptcentre.ie

Abstract

This work is part of ongoing research work that focuses on the linguistic analysis and computational description of five different Sign Languages (SLs), namely Irish Sign Language (ISL), Flemish Sign Language (VGT), Dutch Sign Language (NGT), Spanish Sign Language (LSE), and British Sign Language (BSL). This work will be leveraged to inform the development of sign language (SL) lexicon entries for a Sign Language Machine Translation (SLMT) system. In particular, this research focuses on ISL. We investigate the existence of constructions similar to or equivalent in functionality to gerunds in spoken language, in particular, English. The preliminary findings indicate that in order to interpret if gerund constructions do indeed exist within ISL, further analysis and investigation is necessary, in particular within the domain of aspect and aspectual marking in signed languages.

1 Introduction

Sign languages are articulated using the visual-gestural modality, unlike spoken languages, which use the auditory-vocal modality (Perlman et al., 2018). Sign languages make use of Manual Features (MFs) and Non-Manual Features (NMFs). MFs involve the use of handshapes and their location and movement, and the palm orientation, whereas NMFs make use of the head, eye gaze, facial expressions, and body movement within gestural space (Leeson and Saeed 2012, p. 79).

Despite the significant technological advances in the computational processing of spoken languages, which is supported by extensive scientific research, signed languages have not received nearly as much attention. This issue has resulted in the exclusion of deaf and hard-of-hearing individuals and has further contributed to the marginalisation of a minority group that is already under-resourced due to limited access to language technologies and tools that can effectively facilitate communication (Murtagh et al., 2021). Furthermore, there is a lack of research with regard to gerund constructions in SLs. This research work will involve a comprehensive linguistic analysis of gerund constructions across five sign languages. This research work will provide insight into the role that gerunds play within SLs with regard to the expression of ongoing events and actions as well as the formation of complex sentences.

2 Motivation

This research is part of the SignON project, which is a project concerned with bridging the communication gap between deaf, hard-of-hearing, and hearing individuals across Europe. One of the larger aims of the SignON project is to develop an application that will facilitate the translation between signed and spoken languages using different forms (text, video, and audio). As part of the project objectives, researchers will collaborate to guarantee equity in the dissemination of information and digital content across European societies[1].

This work will inform the development of SL lexicon entries within the SignON project. These

[1] https://signon-project.eu/about-signon/the-signon-project/

lexicon entries will be used within the Natural Language Processing (NLP) pipeline, in the development of a SLMT computational engine. This work is motivated by the lack of efficient SLMT, which is still in its early stages (Shterionov et al. 2022). Recent work within this domain includes the use of Role and Reference Grammar (RRG) and the Sign_A framework to provide SL lexicon entries for an SLMT system. (Murtagh et al., 2022). This work focuses on the development of SL lexicon entries that are robust enough to accommodate SLs (ibid.).

Section 3 will provide a summary of our methodology, data, and tools that are used to facilitate the analysis.

3 Methodology

This initial phase of this research work deals with investigating the existence of gerunds within signed languages, in particular to this research, ISL.

3.1 Data

The Signs of Ireland Corpus (SOI) is used within this research work. The SOI corpus consists of data that is collected from 40 male and female participants from the following part of the Republic of Ireland: Dublin, Cork, Galway, Waterford and Wexford. The participants engaged in two forms of stories: the frog story, which is used for cross-linguistic studies, and a personal story from the participant's life (Leeson et al., 2006).

3.2 Viewing the corpus

ELAN (EUDICO Linguistic Annotator) is used to view the SOI Corpus. ELAN is a software application that facilitates creating annotations for video data. It was developed by the Max Planck Institute for Psycholinguistics, The Language Archive, Nijmegen, The Netherlands (https://archive.mpi.nl/tla/elan) (Wittenburg et al., 2006). The software provides multiple tiers that represent annotations of MFs and NMFs for the ISL sentences being articulated. The SOI corpus is annotated using lexical glossing, which is a method of expressing the meaning of signs using English text. Glosses, which are provided in block capitals, are used to reflect the meaning of a sign or multiple signs in a spoken language (Vermeerbergen, 2006). A manual annotation approach is used for the investigation of gerunds within the data. Section 4 provides an overview of gerunds as linguistic phenomena in English.

4 Gerunds as linguistic phenomena

Gerunds in spoken language, in particular spoken English, present themselves with the suffixation *-ing* at the end of a verb (Huddleston and Pullum 2016, p. 81). Example 1 provides an example of a gerund, where the verb *destroying* includes the suffixation *-ing* (ibid., p. 81).

Example 1

"Destroying the files was a serious mistake."

Biber et al. (1999) provided an account of gerunds in English with many examples. Gerunds may be used as subjects (Example 2(a)), extra-posed subjects (Example 2(b)), subject complements (Example 2(c)), direct objects (Example 2(d)), prepositional objects (Example 2(e)), or complements of preposition (Example 2(f)) (ibid., pp. 201-202).

Example 2

(a) Eating cakes is pleasant.
(b) It can be pleasant eating cakes.
(c) What I'm looking forward to is eating cakes.
(d) I can't stop eating cakes.
(e) I dreamt of eating cakes.
(f) She takes pleasure in eating cakes.

However, additional forms of verbs that use the same suffixation: present participle and past progressive are used with *-ing*. Some verbal nouns and deverbal nouns use *-ing* as one of many forms for nominalisation purposes (Taher 2015). This issue makes the distinction of gerund forms from other forms that use *-ing* suffixation challenging due to the similarity in representation (ibid.).

Leeson and Saeed (2012) refer to constructions in ISL that are equivalent in functionality to gerunds in English. In Example 3(a), the sign PRESENT is used to form the meaning *presenting* in English, whereas in Example 3(b), the reduplication of the sign THINK is used to convey the meaning of *thinking*.

Example 3

(a) HOW YOU (c INDEX f) FEEL FIRST PRESENT
"How did you feel about presenting?"
(Leeson and Saeed, 2012, p. 105)

(b) INDEX+c CANNOT STOP THINK++
"I cannot stop thinking [about it]"
(Leeson and Saeed, 2012, p. 164)

5 Findings

The following examples provide a mapping of ISL translations to English language usage, however, before we can decipher how to define a gerund in terms of signed language and if these examples do indeed reflect instances of gerunds in ISL, we must apply further analysis and investigation.

5.1 Gerunds and classifier constructions

As shown in Example 4, the morpheme "LIFTS" within the construction JEEP-LIFTS-CAR conveys the nominal use of *lifting*.

Example 4

JEEP-HITS-UNDER-CAR JEEP-LIFTS-CAR
'The jeep hit the car, lifting it up'
SOI Corpus Nicholas (22) personal stories (Wexford)

5.2 Gerunds and reduplication of the verb

In ISL, the reduplication of a verb sign may act similarly to verb inflection in spoken languages (Leeson and Saeed, 2012, p. 104). Findings provide instances, where the repetition of a sign can refer to pluralisation. In Example 5, the use of reduplication of the sign BEE serves to pluralise the sign BEE.

Example 5

LOT-OF BEE++ IN DRINK
"Lots of bees in (my) drink."
SOI Corpus Mary (30) personal stories (Cork)

In Example 6(a), the reduplication of the verb sign MEET communicates *meeting*. In Example 6(b), the reduplication of the sign LICK communicates the action of *licking*.

Example 6

(a) INDEX+c* LIVE BEFORE* LIVE RATHMINES INDEX+c* GROW-UP ALWAYS MEET++ DEAF*
"Previously, I lived in Rathmines and grew up always meeting deaf."
SOI Corpus Geraldine (20) personal stories (Dublin)

(b) CONTINUE+ COME-OVER LICK-DRINK LICK++++ INDEX+c DRINK
"(The dog) came over again, licking my drink."
SOI Corpus Eilish (10) Personal Stories (Dublin)

5.3 Gerunds and the citation form of the verb

In Example 7, the sign PLAY is used to express the action of *playing*.

Example 7

CONTINUE BASKETBALL PLAY
"Continue playing basketball."
SOI Corpus Caroline (15) Personal Stories (Dublin)

5.4 -ing suffix in sign language

Sign reduplication and classifier constructions appear to be significantly important with regard to the investigation of gerunds in SL. Example 8 shows some other uses of both. In Example 8(a), the reduplication of the sign RAIN marks an ongoing activity of the verb, accompanied by the sign NOW, resulting in an articulation equivalent in linguistic terms, to the present participle English verb *raining*. Similarly in Example 8(b), the reduplication of the sign WANT marks an ongoing activity of the verb *want*, which it is linguistically equivalent to the present participle verbs *wanting* or *asking* in English. In Example 8(c), the reduplication of the sign EXPLAIN serves as past progressive *explaining* due to the mention of tense at the beginning of the utterance. In the case of classifier construction DOG-SITTING-UP-WITH-PAWS in Example 8(d), the sign SITTING serves as past progressive *sitting*.

Example 8

(a) RECENT DRY* RECENT DRY* BUT RAIN++ NOW RAIN+++
"Recently, it was dry but now it is raining."
SOI Corpus Nicholas (22) personal stories (Wexford)

(b) WANT+++ ALL FOUR CHILDREN WANT ++ MOTHER HELP-ME
"The four children are asking their mother for help."
SOI Corpus Frankie (11) Personal Stories (Dublin)

(c) MOTHER EXPLAIN++ LOW RATHMINES ROAD STRONG LIVE DEAF
"My mother was explaining that the deaf lived in the lower road of Rathmines."
SOI Corpus Geraldine (20) Personal Stories (Dublin)

(d) THAT NIGHT *DOG DOG-SITTING-UP-WITH-PAWS WAIT
"That night, the dog was sitting up with paws, waiting."
SOI Corpus Fiona (36) Frog story (Waterford)

6 Conclusions and future work

We have outlined here our preliminary research towards accommodating gerunds within the sign language lexicon. We have provided a mapping of ISL translations to English language usage. The preliminary findings indicate that to correctly interpret if gerund constructions do indeed exist within signed languages, further analysis and investigation is necessary, in particular within the domain of aspect and aspectual marking in signed languages and spoken languages.

There are many challenging obstacles with regard to the process of identification of these constructions within signed languages. Even if verb reduplication conveys the meaning of an inflected verb with *-ing* (in English), the context determines whether the construction is a present participle construction or past progressive, due to the use of aspect or tense. With regard to SL, in some cases, reduplication refers to pluralisation and does not convey any other meaning (e.g. the repetition of the sign BEE in Example 5, in which it serves as plural (*bees*)).

Future work will focus on gathering more evidence with regard to gerunds within signed languages. Further investigation will be carried out in terms of the morphological characteristics of gerund constructions within signed languages, alongside an analysis of their contextual usage.

Acknowledgment

This project has received funding from the European Union's Horizon 2020 Research and Innovation Programme under Grant Agreement No. 101017255. We wish to acknowledge the School of Linguistic, Speech and Communication Sciences, Trinity College Dublin, and the Centre for Deaf Studies, Trinity College Dublin, for providing us with access to the SOI corpus.

References

Biber, Douglas, Stig Johansson, Geoffrey Leech, Susan Conrad, and Edward Finegan. 1999. Longman Grammar of Spoken and Written English. Harlow: Perason Education Limited.

Chien-hung Lin. 2014. "The Relation of Comparatives to Events in Taiwan Sign Language: A Role and Reference Grammar Account." (2):1–3.

Huddleston, Rodney, and Geoffrey K. Pullum. 2016. The Cambridge Grammar of the English Language. 9th ed. Cambridge: Cambridge University Press.

Leeson, Lorraine, and John Saeed. 2012. *Irish Sign Language: A Cognitive Linguistic Account*. 1st ed. Edinburgh: Edinburgh University Press Ltd.

Leeson, Lorraine, John Saeed, Deirdre Byrne-Dunne, Alison Macduff, and Cormac Leonard. 2006. "Moving Heads and Moving Hands: Developing a Digital Corpus of Irish Sign Language. The 'Signs of Ireland' Corpus Development Project." *Proceedings of Information Technology and Telecommunications Conference, Carlow, Ireland* (Leeson).

Murtagh, Irene. 2019. "A Linguistically Motivated Computational Framework for Irish Sign Language." University of Dublin, Trinity College.

Murtagh, Irene, Rachel Moiselle, and Lorraine Leeson. 2021. "Sign Languages and Language Technology: Linguistic and Technical Challenges." *IRAAL Conference Presentation*.

Murtagh, Irene, Víctor Ubieto Nogales, and Josep Blat. 2022. "Sign Language Machine Translation and the Sign Language Lexicon: A Linguistically Informed Approach." 1:240–51.

Perlman, Marcus, Hannah Little, Bill Thompson, and Robin L. Thompson. 2018. "Iconicity in Signed and Spoken Vocabulary: A Comparison between American Sign Language, British Sign Language, English, and Spanish." *Frontiers in Psychology* 9(AUG):1–16.

Shterionov, Dimitar, Mirella De Sisto, Vincent Vandeghinste, Aoife Brady, Mathieu De Coster, Lorraine Leeson, Josep Blat, Frankie Picron, Marcello Paolo Scipioni, Aditya Parikh, Louis ten Bosch, John O'Flaherty, Joni Dambre, and Jorn Rijckaert. 2022. "Sign Language Translation: Ongoing Development, Challenges and Innovations in the SignON Project." Proceedings of the 23rd Annual Conference of the European Association for Machine Translation 325–26.

Taher, Inam Ismael. 2015. "The Problematic Forms of Nominalization in English: Gerund, Verbal Noun, and Deverbal Noun." English Linguistics Research 4(1).

Vermeerbergen, Myriam. 2006. "Past and Current Trends in Sign Language Research." *Language & Communication* 26(2):168–92.

Wittenburg, P., H. Brugman, A. Russel, A. Klassmann, and H. Sloetjes. 2006. "ELAN: A Professional Framework for Multimodality Research." *Proceedings of LREC*

Association for Computational Linguistics
209 N. Eighth Street
Stroudsburg, Pennsylvania 18360

ISBN 978-1-7138-8994-6
9 781713 889946

CURRAN ASSOCIATES INC.
proceedings.com

1st Workshop on Semiparametric Methods in NLP: Decoupling Logic from Knowledge (Spa-NLP 2022)

Dublin, Ireland
27 May 2022